Strategic Culture Matters

Wilhelm Mirow

The FORSCHUNGSBERICHTE INTERNATIONALE POLITIK are presenting the research results of members and fellows from the *Center for Transnational Relations, Foreign and Security Policy* of the Otto-Suhr-Institute for Political Science at the Department of Political and Social Sciences, Freie Universität Berlin. The reports focus on the foreign and security policies of Germany and the United States of America as well as the larger themes of transatlantic relations and European security. Analysis is based upon a broad understanding of 'security', which encompasses traditional military and defence policy issues as well as new security risks. Various dimensions of international relations relevant to security and governance issues on the state, transnational or international level, such as questions of human rights, economics, culture and identity, are addressed.

Editor's address:

Ingo Peters
Freie Universität Berlin,
Department of Political and Social Sciences
Center for Transnational Relations,
Foreign and Security Policy
Ihnestr. 22, 14195 Berlin,
Phone +49 (0)30 / 838-55530
ingo@zedat.fu-berlin.de

FORSCHUNGSBERICHTE
INTERNATIONALE POLITIK

38

Strategic Culture Matters

A comparison of
German and British military interventions
since 1990

Wilhelm Mirow

LIT VERLAG

Bibliographic information published by the Deutsche Nationalbibliothek
The Deutsche Nationalbibliothek lists this publication in the Deutsche Nationalbibliografie; detailed bibliographic data are available in the Internet at http://dnb.d-nb.de.

ISBN 978-3-8258-1866-1

A catalogue record for this book is available from the British Library

Fresnostr. 2 D-48159 Münster
Tel. +49 (0) 2 51-620 32 22 Fax +49 (0) 2 51-922 60 99
e-Mail: lit@lit-verlag.de http://www.lit-verlag.de

Distribution:

In Germany: LIT Verlag Fresnostr. 2, D-48159 Münster
Tel. +49 (0) 2 51-620 32 22, Fax +49 (0) 2 51-922 60 99, e-Mail: vertrieb@lit-verlag.de

In Austria: Medienlogistik Pichler-ÖBZ GmbH & Co KG
IZ-NÖ, Süd, Straße 1, Objekt 34, A-2355 Wiener Neudorf
Tel. +43 (0) 22 36-63 53 52 90, Fax +43 (0) 22 36-63 53 52 43, e-Mail: mlo@medien-logistik.at

In Switzerland: B + M Buch- und Medienvertriebs AG
Hochstr. 357, CH-8200 Schaffhausen
Tel. +41 (0) 52-643 54 85, Fax +41 (0) 52-643 54 35, e-Mail: order@buch-medien.ch

Distributed in the UK by: Global Book Marketing, 99B Wallis Rd, London, E9 5LN
Phone: +44 (0) 20 8533 5800 – Fax: +44 (0) 1600 775 663
http://www.centralbooks.co.uk/html

Distributed in North America by:

Transaction Publishers
New Brunswick (U.S.A.) and London (U.K.)

Transaction Publishers
Rutgers University
35 Berrue Circle
Piscataway, NJ 08854

Phone: +1 (732) 445 - 2280
Fax: + 1 (732) 445 - 3138
for orders (U. S. only):
toll free (888) 999 - 6778
e-mail: orders@transactionpub.com

Acknowledgements

I would like to give special thanks to Professor Thomas Risse and Dr Ingo Peters of the Freie Universität Berlin, who supervised the work on this book, for the helpful advice and encouragement they provided. My friends Andreea Pavel, Henry Thomson, Daniel Wessnigk, Georg Löfflmann, Christoph Seidler and Martin Waltermann deserve enormous gratitude for many inspiring conversations and discussions. I would also like to thank my parents, Andrea and Harald Mirow, for their loving support during the sometimes difficult hours I spent on completing this book.

"Most students of national security accord pride of place to material forces that define the balance of power between states. They have no patience for intangibles like culture."
-- Peter J. Katzenstein[1]

"Every realist, whatever his profession, is ultimately compelled to believe not only that there is something which man ought to think and do, but that there is something which he can think and do, and that his thought and action are neither mechanical nor meaningless."
-- E. H. Carr[2]

"Rather than obedience or disobedience to an abstract set of stipulative requirements, in times of war what really makes the difference in how a nation state, as a collective identity, 'behaves' is the structure of that nation's history and experience – its strategic culture, if you will."
-- Jean-Bethke Elshtain[3]

---

[1] Katzenstein, Peter J. 1998: "Cultural Norms and National Security: Police and Military in Postwar Japan", Cornell University Press, Ithaca and London, p. 17

[2] Carr, E. H. 1981: "The Twenty Years' Crisis", Palgrave MacMillan, New York and Basingstoke, p. 87

[3] Elshtain, Jean Bethke 1995: "Feminist Themes and International Relations", in Der Derian, James (ed.): "International Theory: Critical Investigations", Macmillan, London and Basingstoke, pp. 349-50

Contents

Index of Tables

List of commonly used acronyms

AWACS	Airborne Warning and Control System
BBC	British Broadcasting Corporation
CDU	Christliche Demokratische Union (Christian Democratic Union)
CSU	Christlich Soziale Union (Christian Social Union)
ESS	European Security Strategy
EU	European Union
EUFOR	European Union Force
FAZ	Frankfurter Allgemeine Zeitung
FDP	Freie Demokratische Partei
GDP	Gross Domestic Product
IFOR	Implementation Force
INTERFET	International Force in East Timor
IR	International Relations
ISAF	International Security Assistance Force
KFOR	Kosovo Force
NATO	North Atlantic Treaty Organization
NBC	Nuclear, Biological and Chemical Weapons
OEF	Operation Enduring Freedom
OAF	Operation Allied Force
PDS	Partei des Demokratischen Sozialismus (Party of Democratic Socialism)
RAF	Royal Air Force
SFOR	Stabilisation Force
SIPRI	Stockholm International Peace Research Institute
SPD	Sozialdemokratische Partei Deutschlands (Social Democratic Party)
UK	United Kingdom of Great Britain and Northern Ireland
UN	United Nations
UNAMIR	United Nations Assistance Mission for Rwanda
UNAMSIL	United Nations Mission in Sierra Leone
UNAVEM	United Nations Angola Verification Mission
UNIFIL	United Nations Interim Force in Lebanon
UNOSOM	United Nations Operation in Somalia
UNPROFOR	United Nations Protection Force
UNTAC	United Nations Transitional Authority in Cambodia

INTRODUCTION

Questions of why states intervene when, where and how lie at the heart of International Relations. Traditionally, scholars pursue quantitative analyses of tangible, material factors to answer such questions. Rationalist theories such as neorealism and neoliberal institutionalism emphasise international factors. Neorealism focuses on a state's position in the international structure of relative power capabilities and institutionalism stresses international institutions such as organisations, regimes or treaties. Liberalism stresses the domestic political constitution of states. Only with the introduction of the constructivist paradigm into International Relations theory at the end of the 1980s intangible factors such as norms, ideas and culture came to the fore. A key problem with traditional models is that they cannot explain why there are differences in states' security policies and levels of interventionism although they have similar capabilities and face similar conditions and constraints in their international environment. Foreign Policy Analysis seeks to explain a country's foreign policy by its domestic sources. In this field of IR a distinction between rationalist and constructivist models applies, too. Bureaucratic Politics model, for instance, analyses the institutional make-up of a state and inter-institutional bargaining. Cultural politics approaches on the other hand focus on national predispositions stemming from cultural sources. Despite the existence of this multitude of theories, models and approaches the question of why states with similar capabilities and under similar systemic conditions behave differently in their use of military force persists. This book argues that while innumerable domestic and international factors determine a state's security policy and its military behaviour and while no military intervention is free from various contextual factors, the concept of strategic culture can be particularly helpful in explaining variations in states' proclivities to use military force.

This is not to say that the concept of strategic culture is the sole key factor that can explain why a state intervened militarily in any particular instance. But the potential explanatory power of intangible factors such as culture, norms and ideas must not be understated either. This becomes apparent in numerous current affairs. In Iraq for instance the US army still struggles to pacify the Sunni triangle after four years despite its vast material, technological and numerical superiority over local militias. In this case it seems as if material capabilities are almost inversely proportional to relative power positions. Little over 100 years ago the British army suppressed rebellions in Iraq by means that are no longer culturally and politically accepted in the UK today. This illustrates the relevance and appropriateness of an analysis of cultural factors and to what extent these can explain the modalities of a state's use of military force.

Both Germany and the United Kingdom of Great Britain and Northern Ireland (UK) are industrialised nations, *de facto* liberal democracies, market economies, member states of the European Union (EU) and of the North Atlantic Treaty Organisation (NATO) and similar in the size of their population and economy. Yet both countries differ in the frequency and intensity with which they use military force abroad. To start, Germany's military expenditure in 2006 was at US$ 36,984 million whereas the UK spent US$ 59,213 million on military expenditure in the same year although Germany's population and GDP are both higher.[1] A glance at military interventions since 1990 would also reveal that British forces intervened more often and the UK deployed more troops abroad than Germany. Unlike Germany, the UK participated in both Gulf Wars 1991 and 2003. It also fought in Afghanistan alongside the US since day one of the launch of Operation Enduring Freedom (OEF) in October 2001. In some instances the British government deployed troops without having consulted the parliament first. In Germany on the other hand parliamentary approval is a requirement for troop de-

[1] Stockholm International Peace Research Institute 2007: "SIPRI Data on Military Expenditure", database online at http://first.sipri.org/non_first/milex.php, all internet sources were checked and last accessed on 31/01/2008.

ployment and debates on these tend to be intense. It seems that the UK is more at ease with the use of military force than Germany is. And it seems that a quantitative analysis of material factors can only provide little explanation for this phenomenon. Therefore the hypothesis arises that British strategic culture allows for a higher frequency and intensity in the use of military force than German strategic culture.

This book seeks to explain different frequencies and intensities in the use of military force by Germany and the UK through a qualitative analysis of each state's strategic culture. It will do so by first outlining the research design of this book with the puzzles to be addressed as well as the hypotheses, variables and selected cases in chapter 1. It will then point out the differences in the UK's and Germany's strategic cultures and their military interventions since 1990 in a comparative case design. For this purpose, chapter 2 will attend to the control variables. Chapter 3 will analyse strategic cultures on the basis of opinion polls. Chapter 4 will then outline British and German military behaviour since 1990. In chapter 5 the book will return to the independent variable. It will attempt to trace decision processes and debates in the run up to and during selected instances of military interventions abroad. These are German and British military engagement in Kosovo in 1999 and Afghanistan since October 2001 as well as the comparative cases of the British military intervention in Sierra Leone in 2000 and the German military intervention in the Democratic Republic of Congo in 2006.

1.) Research design

1.1 Introducing the puzzle

1.1.1 Empirical puzzle

According to former chancellor Helmut Kohl's memoirs former British Prime Minister Margaret Thatcher stated at an EC Summit in December 1989: "We've beaten the Germans twice and now they're back".[1] Although probably the most outspoken, she was by far not the only European head of government who was somewhat uneasy about the thought of a reunified Germany. Many theoreticians as well as practitioners of international relations voiced speculations about the new geopolitical situation in Europe causing Germany to adopt a more assertive role in its foreign, security and defence policy. These concerns were raised even from within Germany. Politicians such as Friedbert Pflüger and intellectuals such as the historian Michael Stürmer feared a backlash of nationalist sentiments in Germany jeopardising the process of European integration and Germany's commitment to multilateralism.[2] Even the later German Foreign Minister Joschka Fischer asserted in 1994:

> " It starts today with the parole „Take more responsibility!", then the first combat missions will take place, there will be the first casualties, the first patriotic rituals will follow, generals will demand more liberties, war heroes will be celebrated again, traditions that were believed to have vanquished long ago will be exhumed, and the return of the primacy of foreign policy, which German nationals longed for desperately will then be allowed to be ‚celebrated'". …".[3]

One reason for the emergence of such concerns may have been that intuitively most predictions about a state's use of military force are made on the basis of the international environment in which it finds itself. The analyst rarely bothers to proceed the other way around, from states' attributes to their behaviour vis-à-vis its international environment. Even more rarely are intangible factors such as values, ideas, identity and culture taken into account in analyses of state behaviour with regard to the employment of military force. This popular omission is unfortunate and misleading. Yet in International Relations scholarship such intuitive approaches are reciprocated, especially in the neorealist literature. Neorealism stresses international systemic and tangible over domestic and intangible, ideational factors in its formulation of causal relationships. With the end of the Cold War prognoses about an unstable era of multipolarity replacing the more stable and secure world under bipolarity emerged in the neorealist literature. John Mearshimer for instance spoke of the 'Balkanisation' of Europe. In his view, Germany's vulnerable geographic position in the centre of Europe provides fertile soil for a resurgence of nationalism.[4] "The problem of containing German power" would emerge once again and counterbalancing it would prove difficult "for much the same reason that an effective counterbalancing coalition failed to form in the 1930s."[5] More moderately, Geoffrey van Orden asserted in 1994 that Germany "may seek to pursue more self-interested

---

[1] Translation by the author, original in German: „Zweimal haben wir die Deutschen geschlagen, jetzt sind sie wieder da"; Kohl, Helmut 2005: "Erinnerungen, 1982 – 1990", Drömer Verlag, Munich, p. 1013

[2] see Pflüger, Friedbert 1994: "Deutschland driftet. Die konservative Revolution entdeckt ihre Kinder", ECON Verlag, Düsseldorf; and Stürmer, Michael 1992: „Die Grenzen der Macht. Begegnungen der Deutschen mit der Geschichte", Siedler Verlag, Munich

[3] Translation by the author, original in German:„Es fängt heute mit der Parole ‚Mehr Verantwortung übernehmen!' an, dann werden die ersten Kriegseinsätze stattfinden, die ersten Toten wird es geben, die ersten vaterländischen Rituale werden folgen, die Generalität wird mehr Freiheiten wollen, Kriegshelden werden wieder heroisiert, längst überwunden geglaubte Traditionen werden exhumiert werden, und die von den Deutschnationalen heißersehnte Wiederkehr des ‚Primats der Außenpolitik' wird dann ‚gefeiert' werden dürfen…" Fischer, Joschka 1994: „Risiko Deutschland", Kiepenheuer & Witsch, Cologne, p. 229

[4] Mearshimer, John 1990: "Back to the Future: Instability in Europe after the Cold War", *International Affairs* 15:1 (summer), p. 25

[5] Mearsheimer 1990, p. 32

policies with its new frontiers and in traditional German areas of influence in Eastern Europe and beyond." Ultimately, it might "aspire to a normal level of great power activity, pursuing national interests which may differ from those of its allies (…)".[6] In a similar vein Kenneth Waltz stated in 1993 that "Germany may ultimately find that reunification and the renewed life of a great power are more invigorating than the struggles, complications, and compromises" of European integration.[7] As it turned out, Germany did not abandon its commitment to European integration at all since reunification. Margaret Thatcher's concerns turned out to be unfounded since the UK employed military force more frequently and intensively than Germany since reunification. As Kerry Longhurst put it: "An appraisal of German security policy more than a decade after the end of the Cold War shows the serious deficiencies in neo-realist prognoses, especially regarding the ability and actual desire of German elites to pursue a more assertive nationally focused 'normal' security policy as Mearsheimer, Van Orden and others have proposed."[8]
Which theory is therefore better suited to explain the difference between Germany's and the UK's employment of military force more than a decade after the end of the Cold War?

1.1.2 Theoretical puzzle

The non-appearance of German foreign, defence and security policy returning to a normal level of great power activity resulting in its military force being employed less frequently and less intensively than the UK's poses the empirical puzzle to be addressed by this book. The corresponding theoretical puzzle is that states, which face similar international systemic constraints and conditions and which are in many other ways quite similar, behave differently in their use of military force. This puzzle does not only pose a challenge to neorealism but also to other theories such as institutionalism or democratic peace theory. All these cannot account for divergences in state behaviour despite similar independent variables at work: the nature of the international system, relative power capabilities, the domestic institutional make-up of the state and its international institutional embedding. This book seeks to demonstrate that Germany and the UK resemble each other in all these aspects and yet they differ in the frequency and intensity with which they resort to the use of force.

---

[6] van Orden, Geoffrey 1991: "The *Bundeswehr* in Transition", *Survival* 33:4 (July-August), p. 352

[7] Waltz, Kenneth 1993: "The Emerging Structure of International Politics", *International Security* 18:2 (Fall) p. 71

[8] Longhurst, Kerry 2004: "Germany and the use of force", Manchester University Press, Manchester, p. 7

1.2 Introducing strategic culture

1.2.1 Genesis and evolution of the concept

Jack Snyder used the term strategic culture for the first time in a study for the RAND Corporation in 1977 on Soviet nuclear strategy. He argued that despite being on the same plane in the international system and similar material capabilities the Soviet Union would not necessarily start from the same premises as the US in its strategic assumptions. Therefore, he argued, one could not simply transfer American assumptions about deterrence and the defensive use of nuclear weapons to the Soviet side but instead "It is useful to look at the Soviet approach to strategic thinking as a unique 'strategic culture'".[9] He further argued that due to its historical experiences of repeated invasions, its authoritarian political structure and the strong role of its military the Soviet Union had a preference for offensive strikes and thus pursued a radically different nuclear doctrine. He did not see the state as a 'black box', as neorealism does, but argued that culture-specific attributes factor into the formation of a state's strategy. Politico-military elites articulate a strategic culture that is a wider manifestation of public opinion socialised into a specifically Soviet way of strategic thinking and „as a result of this socialization process, a set of general beliefs, attitudes, and behaviour patterns with regard to nuclear strategy has achieved a state of semipermanence that places them on the level of ‚culture' rather than mere policy."[10] In the early 1980s scholars such as Colin Gray and David Jones expanded upon Snyder's work. This first generation of scholars on strategic culture continued to focus on differences between American and Soviet nuclear strategy. While this body of research was an innovation in its focus on domestic, cultural origins of security policy, Iain Johnston cites a number of shortcomings. It conceptualised strategic culture too broadly, including such factors as geography, technology, political psychology and even international system structure. As Johnston highlighted, "If 'strategic culture' is supposed to be the product of nearly all relevant explanatory variables, then there is little conceptual space for a non-strategic culture explanation of strategic choice".[11]

Inspired by the rise of constructivism an increasing number of political scientists became interested in the concept of strategic culture during the 1990s. These sought to avoid the tautological pitfalls of the early works and to develop more rigorous analytical models and research designs with strategic culture as an independent variable that is both falsifiable and distinguishable from other variables.[12] One example for these efforts is Johnston's study of Chinese military practice during the Ming dynasty (1368-1644), which came to the conclusion that "China has exhibited a tendency for the controlled, politically driven, defensive use of force that is deeply rooted in the statecraft of ancient strategists and a worldview of relatively complacent superiority".[13] Ironically, Johnston provided a cultural explanation for why China pursues a largely realist foreign policy. In this study Johnston identified two levels of strategic culture existing in parallel to each other: a "symbolic or idealized set of assumptions and ranked preferences" as well as "an operational set that had a nontrivial effect on strategic choice in the Ming period".[14] In the subsequent article "Thinking on Strategic Culture" Johnston spelled out his approach to linking the concept of strategic culture as an independent variable to state behaviour as a dependent variable. He argues that any comparative design on

---

[9] Snyder, Jack 1977: "The Soviet Strategic Culture: Implications for Limited Nuclear Operations" (R2154-AF, Rand Corporation), Santa Monica, p. v

[10] Ibid.

[11] Johnston, Iain 1995b: "Thinking about Strategic Culture", *International Security* 19:4 (Spring), p. 37

[12] Lantis, Jeffrey 2002: Strategic Culture and National Security Policy, in: International Studies Review 4: 3, p. 96; Johnston 1995b, p. 41

[13] Johnston, Iain 1995a: "Cultural Realism - Strategic Culture and Grand Strategy in Chinese History", Princeton: Princeton University Press

[14] Johnston 1995a, p. x

strategic culture must first prove the existence of a consistent and persistent strategic culture within a society, which impacts upon actors' strategic preference rankings. A strategic culture's congruence can be tested through the methods of symbols analysis and cognitive mapping. In Peter J. Katzenstein (editor) *The Culture of National Security* the editor argues that there are two ways in which norms can affect state interests and policies. Norms can "operate like rules that define the identity of an actor, thus having 'constitutive effects' that specify what actions will cause relevant others to recognize a particular identity" or they can have "'regulative' effects that specify standards of proper behaviour."[15] According to Katzenstein, cultural or institutional elements – most often norms – can shape national security interests or the security policies of states directly or they shape identities, which in turn affect national security interests or policies of states.[16] Although generations of scholarship have produced greater understanding of the ties between culture and state behaviour linking these two remains the biggest challenge for researchers in this field to this day.

1.2.2 Defining strategic culture

Before selecting a working definition of strategic culture the meaning attached to several other terms used in connection with this concept must be clarified first. For the purposes of this book the concept of strategic culture consists of at least four component concepts, which all consist of the same immaterial, cognitive substance – thought – but delimit different magnitudes of it. These parts are, in order of magnitude, ideas, norms, identity and culture. Their meanings are all deeply interrelated and interlinked.

The concept of *norms* will be used "to describe collective expectations for the proper behaviour of actors with a given identity".[17] As stated before, these can have regulative or constitutive effects. *Identity*, in turn, is used "as a shorthand label for various constructions of nation- and statehood", which depicts "varying national ideologies of collective distinctiveness and purpose".[18]

This book will adopt a notion of *strategy* in the Clausewitzian tradition as depicting a means-ends complex of state behaviour. It defines the conditions for the employment of military means, the ways in which states make use of military force to advance their interests and the political aims of the use of force.[19]

The meaning of the term *culture* is a more complicated matter as there is dispute over the notion of culture to be employed amongst theorists on strategic culture. After all, when seeking a definition of culture one cannot but choose between the frontlines of the positivist or "explaining"[20] and the "understanding"[21] camp of epistemology. In the literature on strategic culture scholars such as Colin Gray represent the "understanding" camp. This "first generation of theorists on strategic culture"[22] conceptualises culture as context, which means that it cannot be separated from the behaviour of political actors as it comprises the context within which their action has to be understood.[23] Hence, culture can be used to understand the reasons and motives for an action. It cannot be used to explain an action by establishing causal

[15] Katzenstein, Peter J. (ed.) 1996: "The Culture of National Security: Norms and Identity in World Politics", Columbia University Press, New York, p. 5
[16] Ibid, pp. 52 - 53
[17] Katzenstein (ed.) 1996, p. 5
[18] Ibid, p. 6
[19] Dalvi, Sameera: "Germany", in: Glenn, John/Howlett, Darry/Poore, Stuart (editors) 2003: "Neorealism versus Strategic Culture", Ashgate, Aldershot, p. 209; Howard, Michael 1978: "The Forgotten Dimensions of Strategy", *Foreign Affairs* 57: 5 (winter), pp. 975-976
[20] Geertz, Clifford 1973: "The Interpretation of Cultures", Basic Books, New York
[21] Checkel, Jeffrey 1998: "The Constructivist Turn in International Relations Theory", *World Politics* 50: 1
[22] Johnston 1995b, p. 36
[23] Gray, Colin S. 1999a: "Modern Strategy", Oxford University Press, New York and Oxford, 1999

rules about this behaviour. Thus in Gray's definition culture "comprises the persisting (though not eternal) socially transmitted ideas, attitudes, traditions, habits of mind, and preferred methods of operation that are more or less specific to a particular geographically based security community that has had a necessarily unique historical experience"[24]. The third generation of theorists on strategic culture argue that such a definition of culture as context, which includes behaviour, leaves any notion of strategic culture too blurred and renders it overly deterministic[25]. Much rather, culture is seen as a potentially important independent variable, "an ideational milieu, which limits behavioural choices".[26] Similarly, Katzenstein sees culture "as a broad label that denotes collective models of nation-state authority or identity, carried by custom or law. Culture refers to both a set of cognitive standards (such as norms and values) and a set of evaluative standards (such as rules and models) that define what social actors exist in a system, how they operate, and how they relate to one another".[27] These definitions do not include behaviour but assert a causal relationship between culture and behaviour. The third generation of scholarship on strategic culture thus take a positivist stance and seek a notion of culture that allows for strategic culture to be an independent variable that is falsifiable and distinguishable from non-cultural variables.

In this context Johnston defines *strategic culture* as "a system of symbols (e.g. argumentation structures, languages, analogies, metaphors), which acts to establish pervasive and long-lasting strategic preferences by formulating concepts of the role and efficacy of military force in interstate political affairs, and by clothing these conceptions with such an aura of factuality that the strategic preferences seem uniquely realistic and efficacious".[28] Meyer takes a position in the middle ground by realising "Johnston's explanatory aspirations"[29] while still allowing behavioural patterns to be included in the definition, though under the condition that these are "socially transmitted" and "identity derived", without being overly deterministic. He defines strategic culture as "comprising the socially transmitted, identity-derived norms, ideas and patterns of behaviour that are shared among the most influential actors and social groups within a given political community, which help to shape a ranked set of options for a community's pursuit of security and defence goals".[30] This essay will adhere to this definition except for that it will rigorously exclude patterns of behaviour as this would constitute a tautology. It will see strategic culture as a set of norms or ideas collectively held by a society, which influence actors' preferences and behaviour in complex ways. These norms are however neither permanent nor omnipotent. They can change, are occasionally disregarded by some political actors and can be contested within societies. Nevertheless, they are relatively persistent and change only slowly. Violations of norms contained in a strategic culture come at high political costs to decision-makers. Patterns of behaviour can suggest cultural traits but do not necessarily constitute them and cannot stand alone as indicators for a particular culture.

1.2.3 Causal mechanisms

With the bulk of definitions and literature on strategic culture in mind we can now assemble causal mechanisms between strategic culture and state behaviour in the form of the use of military force (military behaviour) for this book. According to the teachings of moderate

[24] Gray, Colin S. 1999b: "Strategic Culture as Context: the First Generation of Theory Strikes Back", *Review of International Studies* 25, p. 51

[25] Johnston 1995b, p. 41

[26] Johnston 1995b, p. 46

[27] Katzenstein 1996, p. 6

[28] Ibid.

[29] Meyer, Christoph O. 2006: "The quest for a European strategic culture: changing norms on security and defence in the European Union", St. Martin's Press, London and New York, p. 20

[30] Ibid, p. 20

constructivism state identities and interests are not exogenous to process.[31] Constructivists stress ideational rather than systemic factors in explanations of state behaviour. In this context, norms are of particular explanatory relevance. They are the product of communicative action, which means that they emerge and evolve through a perpetual process of communication.[32] This can happen through regular social practice, conscious promotion to further specific interests or deliberate negotiation i.e. in conflict management. Ultimately, "State interests and strategies thus are shaped by a never-ending political process that generates publicly understood standards for action."[33] Norms can affect behaviour either through constitutive effects, thereby also acting through identity or directly through regulative effects, whereby a specific identity is presupposed. In the first case they make up a particular identity and in the second case they prescribe actions in line with an actor's identity or prohibit those which are not. In both cases norms generate collective expectations and these have strong causal effects.[34] In fact, collective expectations render norms their causal powers. Essentially, it is collective expectations that help to shape what Johnston termed "a limited, ranked set of grand-strategic preferences", which are, in his view, the main empirical referent of a strategic culture.[35] Also, due to collective expectations any actions, which are not in line with a strategic culture, incur high political costs on the deviator. Therefore norms generating these collective expectations deserve closer scrutiny for explanations of national security policy. The norms held by a particular community constitute its strategic culture and make up its component parts. This book will identify and open up strategic cultures in Germany and Britain to see how norms contained by them differ and how they result in differing identities, collective expectations, and behaviour.

[31] Wendt, Alexander 1992: „Anarchy is what States Make of it: The Social Construction of Power Politics", *International Organization* 46:2 (spring), pp. 391-425

[32] Müller, Harald 1994: "Internationale Beziehungen als kommunikatives Handeln", *Zeitschrift für Internationale Beziehungen* 1:1 (June), pp. 15 – 44; Johnson, James 1991: „Habermas on Strategic and Communicative Action", *Political Theory* 19:2 (May), pp. 181 - 201

[33] Katzenstein 1996, p. 21

[34] Ibid, p. 7

[35] Johnston 1995b, pp. 47 - 48

1.3 Hypothesis generation

With these theoretical tools at hand we can now generate the following hypothesis:
If one can identify at least two distinct strategic cultures these should have a discernible effect on each state's military behaviour or the intensity and frequency with which it uses military force. The higher a strategic culture's proclivity to the use of force (independent variable) the more likely is a state to use military force more frequently and intensively (dependent variable). This book will test this hypothesis on the cases of German and British military interventions since 1990. As this hypothesis presupposes the existence of two distinct strategic cultures, this constitutes a separate hypothesis that must be addressed first.
This book does not hypothesise that strategic culture is a sufficient condition for a state's frequent and intensive use of force but instead hypothesises that a strategic culture with a high proclivity to the use of force is a necessary condition for their frequent and extensive employment by a given state. Politico-military decision-makers may have the power not to act in accordance with their cultural embedding, but this comes at a high political cost.
Neither does the book postulate that strategic culture is a static, exogenously given attribute of a state. It investigates tendencies, which are fundamentally dynamic. A great deal of the literature on German strategic culture argues for instance that it is in a process of change away from strict pacifism towards more interventionism at the moment. Nevertheless this book hypothesises that German strategic culture to this day is more pacifist, which causes Germany to be more reluctant to use military force than the UK.

1.4 Methodology

To empirically test these deductively generated hypotheses this book will utilise a most similar case design research method.[36] However, it is always possible that hitherto unknown independent variables have a direct effect on the dependent variable. In this case it would be possible that variation in one independent variable with all other known variables held constant only correlates with the variation in the dependent variable but does not cause it. In order to render the assumed causal relationship between states' strategic culture and their strategic behaviour in the use of military force more plausible this book will try to reconstruct the causal path from strategic culture to state behaviour as regards the use of military force as completely as possible. This will be done by focusing on public as well as elite opinion and by analysing decision processes and crucial parliamentary debates.

[36] The essential logic of the comparative method is derived from John Stuart Mill's "A System of Logic" (1843), in which he discusses the "method of agreement" and the "method of difference". This book will utilise the latter. See also George, Alexander L./Bennet, Andrew 2004: "Case Studies and Theory Development in the Social Sciences", MIT Press, Cambridge MA.

1.5 Operationalisation

For the central hypothesis to be confirmed strategic culture as an independent variable is to vary between Great Britain and Germany in correlation with their strategic behaviour or their record of the use of military force. A fundamental problem in this endeavour is that strategic culture is an immaterial concept that cannot be measured as easily as more tangible factors such as power capabilities. Therefore they and their expressions need to be clearly defined.

1.5.1 Independent variable

This book will measure the proclivity to the use of force of Germany's and the UK's strategic cultures. Strategic cultures can be distinguished from each other through collective norms. Before its indicators can be determined the possible expressions of this variable need to be established first. A single dichotomy between "weak and "strong" strategic cultures[37] does not suffice. This is because there may be contradictions and trade-offs between different kinds of norms such as a society's loyalty to its allies and its attachment to the use of force for instance. Johnston suggests to classify strategic cultures along a spectrum ranging from soft idealpolitik to hard realpolitik by analysing three vectors of shared assumptions about the use of force: the efficacy of violence, the nature of conflicts (whether these are zero-sum or variable-sum) and the role of war in human affairs (whether it is an aberration of inevitable).[38] Yet this classification does not allow for contradictions between different categories of norms either and may not encapsulate all relevant normative dimensions. Meyer developed the most useful approach by splitting strategic culture into four broad categories of norms. The first addresses "acceptable goals for the use of force", the second concerns states' beliefs about how to engage with other states in the realm of security policy (whether to form alliances or adhere to strict neutrality), the third the degree of internal and international authorisation required for the use of force and the fourth category concerns "the way in which force is used", whether it is used restrictively or excessively (see Table 1).[39] With the help of opinion surveys such as *World Values Survey, Eurobarometer* or *Transatlantic Trends* as well as Meyer's expert opinion surveys[40] strategic norms in the UK and Germany will be compared in each category. One problem with these data sets is that the opinion survey data at hand only represents a small sample of public opinion and does not always ask the perfectly appropriate questions at the appropriate points in time. Also, with public opinion surveys the persistence of a strategic culture from its formative moment to the present cannot be established as the survey data is not available for each year.

[37] As done by Rynning, Sten 2003: „The European Union: Towards a Strategic Culture?" *Security Dialogue* 34: 4, p. 484

[38] Johnston 1995b, p. 46

[39] Meyer 2006, pp. 22 -24

[40] Expert survey based on responses from 31 parliamentarians sitting on national security and defence select committees and 28 experts from national think-tanks. Questionnaires were distributed between June 2005 and September 2005 in the UK, Germany, France and Poland. See Meyer 2006, pp. 189 – 199.

Table 1: Strategic norms concerning the legitimate ends and means of defence policy[41]

	Proclivity to the use of force (1=low, 4=high)			
Values dimensions	1	2	3	4
Goals for the use of force	Territorial defence, reaction to immediate threat	Plus Humanitarian Intervention, aimed at stopping grave violations of human rights	Plus self-serving intervention, related to pursuit of power, material or ideological interests	Plus territorial & political expansion and conquest
The way in which coercive means are used	Restrained and highly proportionate, low risk tolerance vis-à-vis own and foreign casualties	Proportionate, low to moderate risk tolerance regarding own and foreign casualties	Disproportionate, moderate risk tolerance vis-à-vis own, high risk tolerance vis-à-vis foreign casualties	Highly disproportionate, high level of risk tolerance regarding both own and foreign casualties
Preferred mode of cooperation	Neutrality (defensive)	Affiliation with alliances/organisations	Affiliation with particular states	Unilateralism (offensive)
International/ domestic authorisation requirements	High domestic, high international	High domestic, low international	Low domestic, high international	Low domestic, low international

Meyer provides a useful classification of norms that make up a strategic culture but the scale he uses, ranging from one to four, is too crude for the purposes of this book as the variations between Germany's and the UK's strategic cultures are most likely too small to be grasped by this scale. Therefore, it will adopt his values dimensions but not the scale he uses for them. Instead, it will establish Germany's and the UK's position on a spectrum ranging from one end of Meyer's scale to the other in each values dimension.

Another important referent in the study of strategic cultures in addition to broader public opinion are parliamentary debates on the use of military force, the so-called crucial debates. These parliamentary debates voice the opinion of elites rather than the broader public. This distinction is important because elite and public opinion may not always correspond – especially in times of great change when the former reacts immediately and then tries to pull public opinion in their direction. They are thus two distinct bodies of opinion that influence each other in complex ways. The causal path does not go from public to elite opinion alone. Foreign, security and defence policy elites may react to domestic as well as international pressures and are at the forefront of decision-making, thus act as 'gate-keepers' of a strategic culture. In order to ascertain two distinct strategic cultures in the UK and Germany this book will therefore analyse decision procedures and parliamentary debates over military interventions in Kosovo 1999 as well as Afghanistan 2001 and it will compare decision processes and parliamentary debates on the British military intervention in Sierra Leone 1999 with those on the German military deployment to the Democratic Republic of Congo in 2005.

As a useful method to analyse security policy discourses in the study of strategic culture Johnston proposes symbols analysis. This would require the analysis of strategically

[41] Meyer 2006, p. 23

relevant discourses for recurring symbols of strategic culture, "frequently used idioms or phrases, which are axiomatically accepted as valid descriptions of a strategic content" and can thereby "cue certain repertoires of behaviour".[42] But rather than merely analysing these crucial debates for patterns of justifications for the use of force, such as recurring phrases, analogies etc., this book will also take the quantitative dimension of these debates into account. The time and effort spent by politico-military elites on deciding upon and justifying the use of military force before troop deployment will also be seen as relevant. This analysis will be used to check upon the data generated through opinion surveys. But within the scope of this book it is not possible to conduct this analysis very extensively. For this reason the time period will be confined to the post-Cold War period from 1990 until the present rather than starting in 1945.

1.5.2 Control variables

Other independent variables that might potentially explain a state's proclivity to use military force will be drawn from rationalist theories, neo-realism in particular. However, these variables do not represent all possible alternative explanations. It is always possible that hitherto unknown variables or contextual, short-term factors such as recent elections, particular attributes of individual actors etc. have causal effects on the independent variable.

Analysis of the causal role of power from a neo-realist perspective assesses state power by its potential capabilities rather than the actual military equipment it accumulates.[43] Therefore, *relative power capabilities* as an independent variable will be measured by a broad number of indicators such as a state's gross domestic product (GDP), its rank on the human development index (HDI) or its population.

One might argue from a neoliberal institutionalist perspective that a state's *international institutional embedding* might also determine its proclivity to use force since institutions can reduce the potential for conflict. Although this variable overlaps with a subcomponent of strategic culture (see Table 1) it will treat institutional embedding in a purely rationalist rather than a normative framework, as does the subcomponent of strategic culture. On a nominal scale the main institutional allegiances will be spelled out for each state.

Democratic peace theory claims that democracies are more peaceful than non-democracies and that they do not fight each other. Therefore this book will compare each state's system of government, its *domestic institutional make-up*. With the help of the Freedom House Index (FHI) data set, it will rank the degree of democratisation in Germany and the UK.

1.5.3 Dependent variable

The dependent variable, defined as the frequency and intensity of military force employed since 1990, will be measured by comparing each state's military interventions abroad since 1990. It will compare the total number of military interventions, the number of troops deployed with each mission and the tasks and mandates with which troops were equipped in each mission (combative, logistical, medical, civil reconstruction, peacekeeping etc.).

1.5.4 Justification of case selection

Although the independent variable strategic culture has more than two expressions it is not possible to analyse the required number of cases within the scope of this book. A case selection bias can also not be ruled out since case selection took place on the basis of variation on

[42] Johnston 1995b, p. 51

[43] See Baldwin, David 1979: "Power Analysis and World Politics", *World Politics* 31: 2 (January), pp. 161-194

the dependent variable. For these reasons this book will try to render a causal relationship between strategic culture and state behaviour as plausible as possible by outlining as many causal steps from independent to dependent variable as possible. The cases of Germany's and the UK's use of military force since 1990 are chosen mainly because these allow for a high number of other independent variables to be held constant as both countries resemble each other in many ways. Germany and the UK also represent a hard case for the study of strategic culture in two respects. Firstly, the use of military force is the domain of traditional, rationalist approaches to security studies. If a constructivist theory can establish a positive correlation empirically this confers more explanatory powers to constructivism. Secondly, since Germany and the UK resemble each other in many respects, they should be expected to resemble each other in their behaviour as regards the use of military force, too.

2.) Control variables

2.1 Control variable 1: Relative power capabilities

The American psychologist Abraham Maslow once famously stated that if you hold a hammer in your hand you are likely to treat every problem as a nail.[7] This statement reflects a possible neorealist explanation to the empirical puzzle: the UK uses military force more frequently and intensively because it can. According to Kenneth Waltz it is mainly the structure of the international system that determines state behaviour. Structure is characterised by its ordering principles, the attributes of its actors and the distribution of capabilities. The structure of the international political system, in contrast to national political systems, is characterised by anarchy, which entails the permanent risk of a violent attack. Therefore, actors' attributes are functionally the same: the primary task of each state is to provide security to its citizens. The only factor that varies is the distribution of states' capabilities to do so: "States are alike in the tasks they face, though not in their abilities to perform them."[8] As states are facing similar tasks it is only rational to assume that some states employ their means to perform them more than others because of their abilities. And when comparing the UK's and Germany's capabilities to provide security through their material power capabilities in the form of military capabilities, there is indeed a discernible difference.

Table 2: Details of British and German military expenditure

	UK	Germany
Military expenditure in constant (2005) US$ m.[1]	59,213	36,984
Military expenditure in local currency (million)[2]	£ 33,440	30,220 Euro
Expenditure on research and development (million)	£ 2,594 2005/06[3]	1,117 Euro[4]
Proportion spent on research and development, in %	7.8	3.7
Expenditure on personnel (million)	£ 11,255 2005/06, £ 11,204 2006/07[5]	11,781 Euro[6]
Proportion spent on personnel, in %	33.5	39.0

Sources: See footnotes.

Table 2 reveals that the UK does not only spend significantly more money on its military, as stated before, but also that the proportional military efficiency per dollar spent on defence is higher in the UK because in both proportional and absolute terms it spends more on research and development. There are many other indications that the UK has a stronger military than Germany. After all, unlike Germany the UK possesses nuclear weapons. Yet, as table 3

[1] Stockholm International Peace Research Institute 2007, http://first.sipri.org/non_first/milex.php.
[2] Ibid.
[3] UK Ministry of Defence 2007: "UK Defence Statistics 2007", data available online at http://www.dasa.mod.uk/natstats/ukds/2007/c1/table108.html.
[4] Presse- und Informationsamt der Bundesregierung 2006: „Verteidigungshaushalt steigt um 150 millionen", Press release, 23/06/06, available online at http://www.bundesregierung.de/nn_22852/Content/DE/Artikel/2006/06/2006-06-23-verteidigungshaushalt-steigt-um-150-millionen.html.
[5] UK Ministry of Defence 2007, http://www.dasa.mod.uk/natstats/ukds/2007/c1/table103.html
[6] Presse- und Informationsamt der Bundesregierung 2006
[7] "I suppose it is tempting, if the only tool you have is a hammer, to treat everything as if it were a nail." Maslow, Abraham 1966: "The Psychology of Science: A Reconnaissance", Harper, New York, p. 15
[8] Waltz, Kenneth 1979: "Theory of International Politics", McGraw-Hill, Reading (MA) and London, p. 96

shows, the *Correlates of War Project* claims that Germany has even slightly more potential power capabilities than the UK.

Table 3: Composition of national material capabilities in 2001 according to the Correlates of War project

	Germany	UK
Iron and steel production (thousands of tons)	44,803	13,543
Military expenditures (thousands of current year dollars)	26,902,000	34,714,000
Military personnel (thousands)	308	211
Energy consumption (thousands of coal-ton equivalents)	461,815	332,580
Total population (thousands)	82,220	58,832
Urban population (population living in cities with population greater than 100,000; in thousands)	25,390	52,930
Composite Index of National Capability (CINC) score	.027985	.0230077

Source: Singer, J. David/Bremer, Stuart/John, Stuckey 1972: "Capability Distribution, Uncertainty, and Major Power War, 1820-1965", in: Russett, Bruce (ed.): "Peace, War, and Numbers", Sage, Beverly Hills, pp. 19-48; Version 3.02; current data set online at http://www.correlatesofwar.org

This reveals the phenomenon that whereas potentials to possess military power are roughly similar the UK prefers to translate potential into actual military power more than Germany. This leads to the fundamental question of how to account for states that do not want to hold a hammer in their hand, figuratively speaking, despite having the capability to do so. Thereby the potential neorealist explanation to the empirical puzzle in fact only adds to it. In this light one could also interpret Maslow's quote as a statement about the bigger explanatory power of ideational factors relative to material ones. According to the teachings of constructivism physical objects receive their place in social reality through the meaning attached to it. Therefore ideas come causally before the hammer, including ideas about the efficacy of the use of military force. To reverse Maslow, when every problem looks like a nail you want to hold a hammer in your hand. Actors' preferences are not the product of exogenously given structural imperatives but of intersubjective social process.

To conclude, it would be premature to conclude from an analysis of military strength that there is a correlation with the dependent variable because there is no variation in potential power capabilities between Germany and the UK. In addition, military strength does not correlate with within-variations across time on the dependent variable. For instance, the German defence budget was significantly higher in the early 1990s than it is today although Germany used force less frequently and intensely in the early 1990s than today.

2.2 Control variable 2: Degree of democratisation

Some components of Democratic Peace Theory suggest that the more democratic a state, the more irenic it is in its nature. This thought has first been brought forward by Immanuel Kant and was subsequently expanded and modified by numerous Democratic Peace theorists. The original Kantian explanation is that in a republic characterised by a division of powers and democracy the genuinely good will in every citizen is more likely to be translated into and to determine state behaviour.[9] This good will in its purest form causes behaviour to be in the enlightened self-interest, which is in line with the common interest since it adheres to the categorical imperative.[10] Fighting wars is not in this enlightened self-interest. Democracies are therefore more peaceful than non-democracies because rational human beings do not want to fight wars.

The successor of this thought is Republican Liberalism, most prominently represented by Ernst-Otto Czempiel[11] and Andrew Moravcsik.[12] "For liberals," Moravcsik argues, "the configuration of state preferences matters most in world politics – not, as realists argue, the configuration of capabilities and not, as institutionalists ... maintain, the configuration of information and institutions."[13] Republican Liberalism analyses which preferences a democracy is prone to configure and reaches the conclusion that "the more unbiased the range of domestic groups represented, the less likely they will support policies that impose high net costs or risks on a broad range of social actors. Thus aggressive behaviour – the voluntary recourse to costly or risky foreign policy – is most likely in undemocratic or inegalitarian polities where privileged individuals can easily pass costs on to others."[14]

In the case of Germany and the UK it is not possible to explain differences in the use of military force on grounds of differing degrees of democratisation. Both countries are de facto democratic republics. Both are rated "free" with a score of 1.0 by Freedom House's *Freedom in the World* index and ranked similarly high by the Economist Intelligence Unit's *Index of Democracy*, with Germany on rank number 13 and the UK on rank number 32.[15] One could argue that the rate of citizen participation is not similar in all policy fields. In the UK for instance the parliament has less control over the use force than in Germany. Yet this, again, only adds to the puzzle rather than explaining it as it cannot be attributed to democratic deficits in the UK.

---

[9] Kant, Immanuel 1795: "Zum ewigen Frieden: Ein philosophischer Entwurf", in: Höffe, Ottfried (ed.) 2004: „Immanuel Kant, zum ewigen Frieden, Akademie, Berlin

[10] "Act only according to that maxim whereby you can at the same time will that it should become a universal law", Kant, Immanuel 1785, translated by Elington, James W. 1993: "Grounding for the Metaphysics of Morals", 3rd ed., Hackett, Indianapolis, p30

[11] Czempiel, Ernst-Otto 1981: „Internationale Politik. Ein Konfliktmodell", Schöningh, Paderborn

[12] Moravcsik, Andrew 1997: „Taking Preferences Seriously. A Liberal Theory of International Politics", *International Organization* 51:4 (autumn), pp. 513 - 553

[13] Ibid, p. 513

[14] Ibid, p. 531

[15] Freedom House 2007: "Freedom in the World", 16/01/2008, www.freedomhouse.org; Economist Intelligence Unit 2007: "Democracy Index", http://www.economist.com/media/pdf/DEMOCRACY_INDEX_2007_v3.pdf

2.3 Control variable 3: International institutional embedding

If we hold the configuration of information and institutions to matter most in world politics, as institutionalists would, differences in the frequency and intensity with which military force is used could be explained on the basis of differing degrees of international institutional embedding. Institutions can reduce uncertainty and provide information. Thereby they can also reduce the need to resort to military means. After all, one of the most remarkable phenomena in international politics is the achievement of lasting peace in Europe through regional integration in the form of the European Union despite millennia of fatal armed conflicts on this continent. Germany and the UK however largely share the same international institutional embedding. Both countries are NATO, EU, UN, OECD and OSCE members, amongst other international organisations. Probably the only marked difference is that Germany is not a member of the Commonwealth of Nations.

One could argue that the two countries differ in the way in which they operate within these organisations, some with more commitment and enthusiasm than others. However, such specific foreign, security and defence policy behaviour is the subject of the dependent variable. Similarities in membership in international organisations highlight that both countries are similarly advanced in establishing the institutional capacities to reduce uncertainty and information deficits which would otherwise make the use of force more pertinent as a foreign policy instrument.

3.) Opening up strategic culture: four normative categories

3.1 Norms regarding legitimate goals for the use of force

Arguably the most pertinent norm category concerns norms on the legitimate use of military force. Questions regarding legitimate purposes of the use of force are, after all, intensely debated both in Germany and the UK whenever they arise. Norms in this category also vary enormously over time and between different societies. As Finnemore rightly points out for instance it is a fairly recent phenomenon that some predominantly Western societies today regard the safeguarding of individuals in other, distant places from imminent threats as perfectly legitimate. Similarly, it is hardly considered legitimate at all nowadays to wage war for the purpose of collecting debt although would have been considered perfectly legitimate only one hundred years ago.[1] This highlights the causal powers of intangible, ideational factors and therefore also the pertinence of analyses of strategic cultures. Differences between and changes within strategic cultures can have strong implications.

3.1.1 Public opinion

In this category some startling differences between Germany and the UK can be identified in opinion polls. For example, as Table 4 shows, significantly more people in Britain would be willing to fight for their country than in Germany. Table 5 reveals an even more drastic difference: Germans seem significantly less inclined to deem a war justified than the British.

Table 4: "Of course, we all hope that there will not be another war, but if it were to come to that, would you be willing to fight for your country?" (in %, UK 1999 not available)

	UK 1990	D East 1990	D West 1990	D East 1999	D West 1999
No	23	34	43	40	40
Yes	68	40	31	28	37
Don't know	9	26	25	25	18

Source: Inglehart et al. 2006: "World Values Survey", www.worldvaluessurvey.com

Table 5: "Under some conditions, war is necessary to obtain justice" (responses in %)

	UK '04	UK '05	UK '06	**UK '07**	D '04	D '05	D '06	**D '07**
Agree strongly	33	23	22	**23**	7	7	6	**6**
Agree somewhat	36	41	42	**36**	24	22	20	**15**
Disagree somewhat	16	14	14	**16**	30	25	31	**28**
Disagree strongly	14	16	18	**21**	38	45	43	**50**

Source: German Marshall Fund et al. 2007: "Transatlantic Trends", 09/2007, p. 54, www.transatlantictrends.org

As these survey results show, only little more than a third of German respondents, compared to over two thirds in the UK, would be willing to fight for their country in the case of another war. Similarly, less than a quarter of German respondents, compared to almost sixty percent in the UK, agree that under some conditions war is necessary to obtain justice. This implies a wholly different attitude towards the use of military force in the two countries.

Differences also exist in survey questions targeting perceptions on the roles of the army. Table 6 shows that although in both countries the army's role is regarded as "defending the country/the territory", less Germans also see its role as "preparing for wars and fighting". This

[1] Finnemore, Martha 2003: "The Purpose of Intervention", Cornell University Press, Ithaca and London, p. 3

again indicates different perceptions on the use of military force. A survey conducted by the Bundeswehr Institute of Social Sciences reveals that in 2006 30 percent of Germans compared to 12 percent of Britons agreed that "The national armed forces do not have real tasks anymore these days and are actually redundant." In the UK, 72 percent disagreed strongly; in Germany 43 percent.[2] Similarly, the survey reveals that only 30 percent of Germans compared to 62 of Britons feel gratitude for their armed forces and only 47 percent of Germans compared to 68 percent in the UK agree that their armed forces have proven themselves to be useful.[3] There seem to be stronger reservations towards the use of force in Germany.

Table 6: Opinions of Europeans about the roles of the army (answers in % "yes" by country)

	D	UK
Defending the country / the territory	95	96
Preparing for wars and fighting	76	93
Keeping or re-establishing peace in the world	75	82
Defending values, such as freedom and democracy	70	76
Passing on to young people values such as discipline, respect for their superiors	44	67
Helping young people to integrate into society e.g. by teaching them a trade	48	63
Guaranteeing/symbolizing national unity	52	61
Helping our country in case of a disaster	91	89
Helping other countries in case of a disaster	80	81
The army is of no use (Spontaneous answer)	6	9

Source: Mannigart, Phillippe et al. 2001: "Europeans and a Common Security and Defense Policy: Technical Report (Tables)", Royal Military Academy, Brussels, p. 5

Different perceptions on the utility of military force do not indicate that Germans feel less exposed to international threats than the British. Much rather, they indicate different preference rankings over effective means to counter them or different perceptions over the efficacy of military force. Threat perceptions are, in fact, quite similar. When asked to name the three main challenges and threats confronting the world, 52 percent in both countries picked international terrorism, 63 percent in Germany and 57 percent in the UK chose environmental destruction and climate change, poverty and overpopulation was chosen by 50 percent in Germany and 56 percent in the UK, religious conflicts and fundamentalism by 36 percent in Germany and 39 percent in the UK, war by around a third and weapons of mass destruction by around a quarter of respondents in both countries.[4] These similarities can also be observed in other data sets. According to *Transatlantic Trends* 2005, when asked to rate the importance of international terrorism as a threat 95 per cent of Germans and 93 per cent of Britons rated it as extremely important or important. The *Special Eurobarometer 54* survey also compared the fears of Europeans for a certain number of threats in 2001 and did not reveal any marked differences.[5]

Similarities in threat perceptions notwithstanding, norms regarding legitimate goals for the use of force differ. To illustrate, whereas 87 percent in Germany and 85 percent in the UK believe that "the European Union (EU) should take greater responsibility for dealing with

[2] Translation by the author, original in German: „Die [nationalen] Streitkräfte haben in der heutigen Zeit keine richtigen Aufgaben mehr und sind eigentlich überflüssig." Sozialwissenschaftliches Institut der Bundeswehr 2006a: „Einstellungen der Bundesbürger zu zentralen sicherheits- und verteidigungspolitischen Fragen", April 2008, last accessed 30/11/2008, p. 29, www.sowi.bundeswehr.de

[3] Sozialwissenschaftliches Institut der Bundeswehr 2006b: "Forschungsbericht 84", April 2008, last accessed 30/11/2008, p. 85, www.sowi.bundeswehr.de

[4] Bertelsmann Foundation 2007: "Who Rules the World?", 22/10/2007, p. 26, www.bertelsmann-stiftung.de

[5] Mannigart 2001, p. 4

these sorts of threats"[6] only 16 percent of Germans compared to 35 percent of Britons agree that the EU should "commit more troops for combat actions" as a means to deal with these threats.[7] This indicates that Germans assign the use of military force a lower position in their preference rankings regarding security policy options than the British. Though to a lesser degree, these different preference rankings also apply to norms regarding the use of military force for humanitarian purposes. In response to the question "Let's imagine an authoritarian regime in which there is no political or religious freedom. To help democracy, would you support sending military forces to remove authoritarian regimes?" only 28 per cent of Germans compared to 40 per cent in the UK answered "yes".[8]

Different norms can result in different identities through constitutive effects. If a strategic culture contains norms more accommodating of the use of military force its society may also identify itself more as a major power responsible for ensuring peace and stability throughout the world. Opinion survey data seems to confirm this. According to the Bertelsmann Foundation, to the question "In your opinion, which of the following countries and organizations are world powers today?" 74 percent of British respondents consider themselves a world power, compared to 49 percent of Germans considering Germany a world power. This is in line with Tony Blair famously describing the UK as a "pivotal country".[9] And to the question if they see their own country as a world power in 2020 64 percent of British respondents answered "yes", compared to 46 percent in Germany.[10]

Table 4 shows that throughout the 1990s there have been no significant changes in German attitudes about defending their country, which highlights persistence in their strong reservations about the use of force. However, other surveys indicate that norms concerning legitimate goals for the use of force changed slightly to become more supportive of German military interventions abroad in the early 1990s. According to the *Institut Allensbach*, in 1988 44 % of the respondents were against Bundeswehr participation with UN peacekeeping operations to monitor ceasefires and agreed that „Especially we Germans should be particularly restrained on such matters due to our past". 36 percent agreed to the opposite claim that "A country of the significance of the Federal Republic cannot simply abdicate from its international political responsibilities" and "Germany must be prepared to take on responsibility also internationally". Already in 1993 the proportion of those against the former and for the latter claim changed to 31 and 54 percent respectively.[11] Similarly, 24 percent of West-Germans and 19 percent of East-Germans favoured creating the preconditions to let Bundeswehr soldiers participate in UN missions in October 1990, whereas 55 percent in West Germany and 53 percent in East Germany were against this.[12] In 1996 already 56 percent in West Germany and 42 percent in East Germany were in favour of German participation in UN peacekeeping operations.[13] This all suggests that German strategic culture changed somewhat to encompass "softer" goals for the use of force such as peacekeeping, although norms changed more in West Germany.

---

[6] German Marshall Fund et al. 2007: "Transatlantic Trends", 07/09/05, 31/01/08, p. 22, www.transatlantictrends.org

[7] Ibid, p. 25

[8] German Marshall Fund et al. 2005, p. 50

[9] Mangold, Peter 2001: "Success and Failure in British Foreign Policy", Palgrave, Basingstoke, p. 96

[10] Bertelsmann Foundation 2007, pp. 17 – 18

[11] Translations by the author, originals in German: „Gerade wir deutschen sollten uns angesichts unserer Vergangenheit bei solchen Fragen besonders zurückhalten", "Ein Land von der Bedeutung der Bundesrepublik kann sich nicht einfach seinen weltpolitischen Verantwortungen entziehen" and „Deutschland muss bereit sein auch international Verantwortung zu übernehmen". Noelle-Neumann, Elisabeth/Köcher, Renate (ed.) 1997: „Allensbacher Jahrbuch der Demoskopie", 1993 – 1997", Verlag für Demoskopie, Allensbach, p. 1144; quoted in Hellmann 2005, p. 178

[12] Noelle-Neumann, Elisabeth/Köcher, Renate (ed.) 1993: „Allensbacher Jahrbuch der Demoskopie", 1988 – 1992", Verlag für Demoskopie, Allensbach, p. 961; quoted in Hellmann 2005, p. 198

[13] Ibid.

3.1.2 Elite opinion

Meyer's Survey of Parliamentarians and Experts[14] suggests some puzzling differences in norms regarding legitimate ends for the use of force. Paradoxically, German security and defence policy elites seem more supportive of using of force for humanitarian purposes than British elites (see tables 7a and 7b). For instance, in Germany 22 percent more experts agreed that military force should be used to liberate people from oppressive regimes, if necessary. Table 7c shows that when it comes to the use of force for non-humanitarian purposes, such as the pre-emptive pursuit of security interests, German and British elites seem to have roughly the same opinion, in contrast to the general public of these two countries.

Table 7a: When necessary, military force should be used to stop human suffering and death in third-countries.

	Strongly agree	Agree, but…	Disagree, but…	Strongly disagree
Germany	71 %	14 %	14 %	0 %
UK	20 %	40 %	40 %	0 %

Table 7b: If necessary, one should use military force to liberate people from oppressive regimes.

	Strongly agree	Agree, but…	Disagree, but…	Strongly disagree
Germany	29 %	43 %	29 %	0 %
UK	0 %	50 %	25 %	25 %

Table 7c: One should not shy away from using military force pre-emptively outside the EU to effectively counter some kinds of threats

	Strongly agree	Agree, but…	Disagree, but…	Strongly disagree
Germany	14 %	71 %	14 %	0 %
UK	22 %	66 %	0 %	11 %

Table 7d: Civil capacities are much better suited than military capacities to preserve and promote peace in the world.

	Strongly agree	Agree, but…	Disagree, but…	Strongly disagree
Germany	17 %	68 %	17 %	0 %
UK	0 %	38 %	50 %	12 %

Table 7e: If you compare your assessment of TODAY to your views in 1990/91, i.e. about 15 years ago, to what extent do the following relative statements apply to you? "I have become much more disposed to regard the use of force as legitimate for the protection of foreign civilians under military prosecution."

	Strongly agree	Agree, but…	No change	Rather the opposite	Completely the opposite
Germany	14 %	57 %	29 %	0 %	0 %
UK	22 %	44 %	22 %	11 %	0 %

Source: Meyer 2006, p. 194

Even more paradoxically, this affirmation to the use of force by German elites, especially for humanitarian purposes, does not seem to result in similar preference rankings amongst German and British security policy elites. As Table 7d shows, 85 percent of German respondents, compared to 38 in the UK, prefer civil over military capacities to pursue certain security policy objectives. It seems as if German security policy elites are double-minded. They maintain norms in line with a civilian power[15] identity while at the same time increasingly adopt-

[14] Meyer 2006, pp. 189 - 199

[15] This book adheres to Hans Maull's definition of a civilian power as "a state that seeks to pursue its foreign and domestic objectives primarily through political and economic means, and which is committed to multilateral co-

ing norms affirming the use of force for humanitarian purposes or the pursuit of vital security interests. This quasi-schizophrenia places German security policy elites increasingly at odds with the German public, which, as argued in section 2.1.1, deems the use of military force illegitimate for almost any goal in its norms. Former German foreign minister Joschka Fischer getting hit by a paint bomb at a *Bündnis 90/Die Grünen* (Green Party) conference in Bielefeld on 15 May 1999 could be seen as an expression of this.[16] The German and the British public differ in their norms concerning legitimate goals of the use of force. German and British security policy elites differ in this norm category only insofar as German elites appear more contradictory. As we will see in section 2.3, this may partly derive from a conflict between preferences generated by the German security policy elite's norms regarding international responsibilities and collective expectations generated by the German general public's norms regarding legitimate goals for the use of force. In the UK norms regarding legitimate goals for the use of force seem more at harmony between elites and the general public. Both assign the use of military force a relatively high position in preference rankings regarding various instances in which the use of military force could be an option. This all indicates that in a democracy humanitarian interventions require decision-makers sympathetic to this cause as well as a society whose norms are compatible with the use of military force for humanitarian ends. Decision-makers need to find a compromise between public attitudes and their own views unless they are willing to pay enormous political costs.

Table 7e shows that there has been a dramatic change in elites' norms since 1990 in favour of the use of force for humanitarian purposes in both countries, and slightly more so in Germany, which suggests that readiness to pursue humanitarian interventions has increased since then.

---

operation and strengthening international law. It is expected to use military force only as a last resort, after the economic instruments of statecraft have failed. Even then, civilian powers are expected only to use military force multilaterally, on the basis of international law, and in a manner proportionate to the political goals." Quoted in Hyde-Price, Adrian 2001: "Germany and the Kosovo War", *German Politics* 10:1 (April), pp. 31-32.

[16] See Fischer, Joschka 2008: „Die Rot-Grünen Jahre: Deutsche Außenpolitik vom Kosovo bis zum 11. Dezember", Droemer Knaur, Munich, p. 222

3.2 Norms regarding the way in which coercive means are used

This norm category is closely related to the previous dimension. A strategic culture that glorifies the sacrifice of its own troops and enemy casualties is not likely to consider the use of force illegitimate for many reasons. It is also a significant component of a strategic culture. History witnessed enormous variations in norms about the ways in which military force should be used across time and cultures, ranging from imperial Japan and Nazi-Germany in the late 1930s and early 1940s to norms in Germany and Japan in the decades subsequent to their defeat for instance. Whereas the former encouraged the maximisation of enemy casualties and dieing for either country was considered heroic the latter is guided by the belief that force should only be used as a last resort, after all other means have been exhausted, and even then only with a maximum degree of restraint for both one's own troops and the enemy.

In this norm category analyses of both public and elite norms are relevant because elites are assumed to be well aware of collective expectations regarding casualties. Elites may also be embedded into their cultural context, which is why the elites' as well as commonly held norms cause strategic culture to affect behaviour in state security and defence matters.

3.2.1 Public opinion

Public opinion surveys indicative of norms in this category are scarce. Unfortunately, the *People on War* survey published by the International Committee of the Red Cross does not include Germany but survey results for the UK, especially inter-temporal comparisons, are also revealing. Asked in 1999 what soldiers should do when combatants attack to weaken the enemy 72 percent replied they should "attack only combatants and leave civilians alone". This figure decreased to 51 percent in 2007. 26 percent in 1999 and 42 percent in 2007 replied instead that they should "attack combatants and avoid civilians as far as possible".[17] This indicates that a preference for the use of force with a maximum degree of restraint to spare civilian casualties diminished significantly in the UK between 1999 and 2007.

Public opinion surveys reveal differences in the prestige attached to the military. Table 6 showed for instance that less than half of Germans compared to two thirds in the UK see it as an important role of the army to promote values such as discipline and respect and when asked how much trust they have in certain institutions only 66 percent in Germany compared to 83 percent in the UK answered they "tend to trust" the army. Table 8 confirms the latter.

Table 8: "Could you tell me how much confidence you have in the armed forces?" (in %)

	UK 1990	UK 1999	D West '90	D East '90	D West '99	D East '99
A great deal	32	27	6	1	6	4
Quite a lot	49	55	34	13	48	40
Not very much	15	14	43	43	34	41
None at all	4	3	17	43	6	10
Don't know	0	2	0	0	5	5

Source: Inglehart et al. 2006

These results may also suggest that there are differences in public attitudes towards ways in which military force should be used. If the military enjoys less prestige in Germany this may indicate that casualties are considered less as something heroic. A less militaristic society is less inclined to accept casualties. This causes German political decision-makers to be more

[17] ICRC 2007: "People On War 2007 Country Report: Great Britain", 12/12/07, p. 11, www.icrc.org

wary of exposing German troops to risky combat situations. Table 8 also suggests that as the German public's confidence in the armed forces increased slightly throughout the 1990s it may have become more inclined to accept the use of force and potentially also the sacrifice of soldiers for humanitarian purposes as legitimate, but still significantly less so than in the UK.

3.2.2 Elite opinion

As table 9a shows, there is indeed a strong difference in the extent to which risks regarding own casualties factor into decisions to deploy military force. In Germany 72 percent of respondents agree that the use of force should be contingent upon low risks of own casualties, compared to 22 percent, the same number that strongly disagrees, in the UK. Table 9b focuses on the concern to avoid foreign casualties. Interestingly, British expert respondents seem significantly more concerned about foreign casualties. German experts seem ambiguous.

Table 9a: Military force should only be deployed, if the risk for your country's troops to sustain casualties is small.

	Strongly agree	Agree, but...	Disagree, but...	Strongly disagree
Germany	29 %	43 %	29 %	0 %
UK	11 %	11 %	56 %	22 %

Table 9b: When military force is employed, it should be done with the maximum restraint, even if this is likely to prolong a given mission significantly.

	Strongly agree	Agree, but...	Disagree, but...	Strongly disagree
Germany	14 %	43 %	43 %	0 %
UK	50 %	38 %	0 %	12 %

Source: Meyer 2005, pp. 191 – 192

These questions go to the heart of a country's ability to deploy troops. Their replies confirm previous results. British decision-makers as well as the British public seem less restrained on questions regarding the use of military force. In Germany on the other hand security policy elites are confronted with two conflicting public expectations. Norms regarding the protection of civilians from immanent threats as legitimate generate some public acceptance of humanitarian interventions. Attitudes of antimilitarism and, in particular, norms regarding ways in which force should be used demand restraint. Germany shows little acceptance of casualties, especially one's own. The Schröder government's fierce rejection of sending ground troops into Kosovo before air strikes in 1999 are but one example of how its strategic culture only allows for military force to be used restrictively, if it is deployed at all.[18] Humanitarian interventions are facing a mediatised dilemma in all Western societies. On the one hand the "CNN-Effect" generates feelings of compassion and collective expectations from governments to "do something". On the other hand, the "body bag effect" demands low casualties. In Germany the conflict between these effects plays out particularly strongly. In most cases, the latter prevails.

[18] Cohen, Roger 1999: "Schroeder's Blunt 'No' to Ground Troops in Kosovo Reflects Depth of German Sensitivities", *New York Times*, 20/05/99

3.3 Norms regarding international co-operation:

Norms on the preferred mode of defence co-operation can also have strong effects on security policy. A strong attachment to multilateralism in Germany for instance may be constitutive of its civilian power identity and may have been responsible for the popular uproar after the German government's decision to join Operation Allied Force (OAF) in May 1999. A strong British attachment to the US may be constitutive of its identity as a transatlantic bridge between Europe and America. This may have played a strong role in shaping former British Prime Minister Tony Blair's decision to join Operation Iraqi Freedom in March 2003.

3.3.1 Public opinion

Yet the picture displayed by public opinion surveys does not entirely match stereotypical images of British and German traditional attachments and entanglements regarding security policy. There are some differences but also astonishing similarities in this norm category.
One interesting finding by the Bertelsmann foundation reveals that the British are more in favour of power politics than Germans, which are more in favour of UN-multilateralism. Thus, to the question within which framework peace and stability in the world can best be achieved 66 percent of German and 47 percent of British respondents answered "a system led by the United Nations". 44 percent in the UK and 20 percent in Germany on the other hand answered "a system led by a balance of regional powers." Notably, of all nine countries addressed by the survey German respondents were most in favour of UN multilateralism.[19]
Somewhat unsurprisingly, as both countries are old hands at NATO, neither country's people see it as particularly committed to neutrality. Thus, 55 per cent in Germany and 64 per cent in the UK see NATO as still essential to their country's security.[20] However, contrary to stereotypes about British Euroscepticism both countries show a strong attachment to the EU in security and defence affairs, although more so in Germany. 86 percent in Germany and 71 percent in the UK deem it desirable that the EU exerts strong leadership in world affairs. Sentiments of attachment to the US on the other hand have weakened steadily in both countries. In 2002 68 percent of German and 72 percent of British respondents deemed it desirable that the US exerts strong leadership in world affairs. In 2007 these figures were reduced to 38 percent in Germany and 50 percent in the UK.[21]. Developments in Iraq might have contributed significantly to these results. The Standard Eurobarometer 64 survey also reveals a clear majority in both countries in favour of a common European security and defence policy although the number is higher in Germany than in the UK (59 % in the UK and 87 % in Germany)[22]. Therefore, although Britons are traditionally more attached to the US and less to the EU than Germans, there is a majority in favour of more EU involvement and a trend away from the US in both countries. The German public shows slightly more normative attachment to UN multilateralism and slightly less normative attachment to the US than the British public.

3.3.2 Elite opinion

Amongst foreign policy elites, the contrast between a more transatlantic and a more European orientation in defence cooperation is stronger. As table 10 shows, although both countries'

[19] Bertelsmann Foundation 2007, p. 38
[20] Transatlantic Trends 2007, p. 34
[21] Transatlantic Trends 2007, pp. 3 – 6
[22] EU Directorate General Communication 2005: "Standard Eurobarometer 64", December, p. 104
http://ec.europa.eu/public_opinion/index_en.htm

elites view the US as their country's closest friend the majority of British elites disagree that Europe should take a more independent approach from the US in security policy matters.[23]

Table 10a: The United States is my country's closest friend and shares most of its values and beliefs.

	Strongly agree	Agree, but…	Disagree, but…	Strongly disagree
Germany	29 %	57 %	14 %	0 %
UK	12 %	75 %	12 %	0 %

Table 10b: Europe should try to become more effective in opposing the US on foreign policy if its values and beliefs are at stake

	Strongly agree	Agree, but…	Disagree, but…	Strongly disagree
Germany	0 %	50 %	50 %	0 %
UK	0 %	28 %	28 %	43 %

Source: Meyer 2006, p. 192

This contrast between British elites loyal to the US and a public drifting away from traditional attachment to the US in security and defence affairs creates a friction that was most visible in the run-up to the war on Iraq in 2003. An explanation for this discrepancy between elites and the public in the UK could be that norms regarding international cooperation are more resistant to change and more persistent for elites since they are reinforced by elite socialisation. In Germany the discrepancy between traditional normative attachment to the US and recent demands for a more independent European security policy is located within elites, not between elites and the public.

[23] Meyer, page 192

3.4 Norms on international and domestic authorisation requirements for the use of force

Norms in this category can be both constitutive and regulatory as they prescribe ways in which the use of force is legitimised and define which authorities a state adheres to. Frequent references to international and domestic law in German debates over troop deployment for instance could be seen as constitutive of its civilian power identity. At the same time, the *kein Alleingang* maxim prescribes that international approval is the proper way to enact a civilian power identity. Similarly, Britain's world power identity could demand a certain level of concern for developments abroad and determination to intervene militarily if deemed necessary, with or without public and international approval.

3.4.1 Public opinion

Yet again, surveys surprise through their defiance to prejudices about Germans and the British. Whereas 41 percent agree strongly and 35 percent agree somewhat to the claim that "The use of force is more legitimate when the United Nations (UN) approves it" only 23 per cent of Germans agree strongly and 37 percent agree somewhat.[24] UN approval to the use of force seems to be of great importance in both countries and even more so in the UK. This might be due to differences in the first norm category: Germans are less inclined to deem the use of force legitimate than the British, with or without UN approval.

Table 11 suggests a similar conclusion. Considering the notorious Euroscepticism amongst the British public it surprises that, although low in both countries, agreement to this statement is fractionally higher in Britain.[25] This suggests a higher proclivity to consider the use of force legitimate as well as lower authorisation requirements in British strategic culture. German antimilitarism prevails over its enthusiasm for European integration and conversely, Britain's strategic culture seems to cause its euroscepticism to recede somewhat when it comes to security and defence policy. After all, the European Security Strategy of 2005 bears quite a British handwriting.[26]

Table 11: "If the European Union should decide to use military force, (Germany/the UK) should abide by that decision, even if (Germany/the UK) disagrees".

	Agree strongly	Agree somewhat	Disagree somewhat	Disagree strongly	Don't know/refusal
Germany	8 %	25 %	32 %	33 %	2 %
UK	14 %	25 %	23 %	34 %	4 %

Source: Transatlantic Trends 2006, p. 9

3.4.2 Elite opinion

However, once again one can witness a difference between the general public and foreign policy decision makers: table 12a shows that in the UK a quarter of experts disagreed with the primacy of international law and the UN while in Germany all agreed.[27] This discrepancy has to be seen in connection with norms about domestic authorisations of the use of force. In a

[24] Transatlantic Trends 2005, p. 30

[25] Transatlantic Trends 2006, p9. See Table 3

[26] One of its main authors was Robert Cooper, Tony Blair's former foreign policy adviser. See Brown, Chris 2004: "Britain and the European Security Strategy", European Foreign Policy Research Network Working Paper No. 6, 08/07/04, last accessed 31/01/08, http://fornet.info/documents/Working%20Paper%20no%206.pdf

[27] Meyer 2005, p. 149, see also table 10a

sense constitutional designs are already an indicator of such a norm being institutionalised. The use of force is strictly subordinated to domestic and international law in Germany ever since the end of the Second World War. It was only in 1994, after a landmark decision by the constitutional court, that a German participation in international combat missions was deemed compatible with the German Basic Law as long as the German parliament approves of it.[28] In the UK it is strictly speaking not a legal requirement that the British parliament is consulted before troop deployment although this is increasingly becoming a code of practice. While there is no data available on public opinion about the role parliaments should play in authorising the use of force expert opinion largely reflects these institutionalised norms. Table 12b reveals stark differences between German and British expert opinion over domestic and parliamentary authorisation requirements.[29] However, Iraq can be argued to be a turning point in British politics as regards the role of public opinion in foreign policy. As Meyer argues, "… we are seeing a remarkable change in British strategic culture towards higher authorisation requirements, which will make it much harder in the future to ignore both international law and domestic opposition"[30]. Though it remains to be seen whether this is the case, it seems unlikely that any future British prime minister will want to face the same kind of anger and blame former Prime Minister Tony Blair received before and after the launch of Operation Iraqi Freedom. In the case of Germany one might argue that there is growing fatigue about parliamentary debates on troop deployments. Nevertheless, since 71 percent of German experts support high domestic authorisation requirements, is unlikely that the strong level of parliamentary control over troop deployment is going to weaken any time soon. So although there might be a convergence towards parliamentary control over armed forces and towards a strong attachment to the UN in both countries fundamental differences over the degree of readiness to use force without public, parliamentary and UN approval remain.

Table 12a: "The use of military force can only be authorised when it is backed up by International law and the authorisation of the United Nations Security Council"

	Strongly agree	Agree, but…	Disagree, but…	Strongly disagree
Germany	43 %	57 %	0 %	0 %
UK	25 %	50 %	25 %	0 %

Table 12b: "Troops can only be deployed if a solid majority in my parliament as well as in public opinion is supporting such a decision by the government"

	Strongly agree	Agree, but…	Disagree, but…	Strongly disagree
Germany	57 %	14 %	29 %	0 %
UK	12 %	25 %	63 %	0 %

Source: Meyer 2005, p. 193

[28] Hellmann, Gunther et al. 2005: „Deutsche Außenpolitik", VS Verlag, Frankfurt am Main, p. 198

[29] Ibid.

[30] Hellmann, p. 152

3.5 Summarising and synthesising the findings

While it is difficult to draw an accurate and comprehensive picture of strategic culture for each country without employing a fair amount of speculation and while opinion polls can only serve as benchmarks a few things have become clear from this analysis.

One striking finding is that German strategic culture shows a lower proclivity to consider the use of force legitimate for a variety of goals. Most strikingly, while around 60 percent of British respondents think that war is sometimes necessary to obtain justice, an overwhelming majority in Germany disagrees, half even strongly. Although German experts and decision-makers strongly support the idea of humanitarian intervention they assign non-military means higher positions in preference rankings for security and defence policy options, which shows that strategic culture factors into their preference formation.

Similarly striking is that, although no perfectly indicative public opinion surveys could be found on this matter, British and German elites fundamentally differ in norms concerning ways in which force should be used, with German elites showing a preference for minimising risks of own casualties.

As regards norms on preferred modes of international cooperation the German public shows a slightly stronger preference for UN multilateralism over power politics than the British public. There are also different preference rankings for EU and transatlantic defence cooperation, with Germany more in favour of defence cooperation at EU level and the UK more in favour of transatlanticism. But this difference is surprisingly small and converging. However, it is still very present amongst security and defence policy experts and decision-makers.

The German and British public view the UN as an important source of legitimacy for military interventions, but more so in the UK than in Germany. Since German strategic culture shows strong attachment to UN multilateralism this indicates a lower proclivity to deem the use of force justified rather than lower international authorisation requirements in Germany. Both countries' norms on the use of force demand UN approval but in Germany this is still no guarantee for public approval to the use of force. Elites in Germany also value UN approval slightly higher than British elites although an overwhelming majority in both countries claims that UN approval is actually vital. Domestic authorisation requirements are significantly lower in Britain than in Germany, both de jure and in expert opinion.

All in all, the findings strongly suggest that German strategic culture shows a lower proclivity to the use of force than British strategic culture. This confirms the preliminary hypothesis that there are two distinct strategic cultures in Germany and the UK. This distinctness does not imply that strategic cultures remain constant over time. Although it is not the main subject of this book this chapter pointed out indications that since 1990 German strategic culture changed towards a slightly higher proclivity to the use of force.

The graphs below merely aim to sketch out and illustrate the findings for each norm category by placing British and German strategic culture along the spectrum proposed by Meyer. It is a subjective generalisation and the findings actually have to be interpreted more delicately.

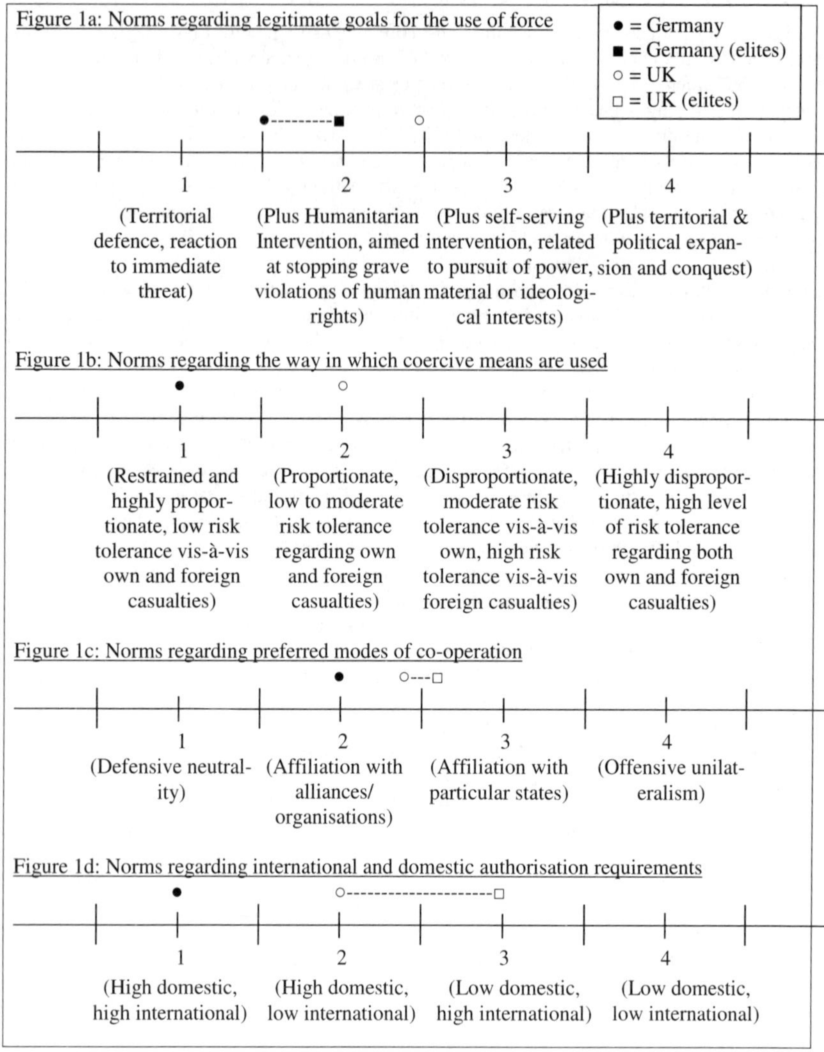

If the mean values of each country in each category are added together, we reach a total degree of proclivity to the use of force of 5.75 for German strategic culture and 9.5 for the UK's on a scale ranging from 0 to 16. This estimate is problematic as these numbers are subjective estimates and norm categories one and two are probably more weighty components of a strategic culture than the other two. Nevertheless, they depict that opinion polls reveal two distinct strategic cultures in Germany and the UK.

4.) British and German military interventions abroad since 1990

Having opened up and analysed strategic cultures in Britain and Germany we can now hypothesise that German strategic culture generates stronger preferences for non-military means as Germans are less inclined to consider the use of military force justified. Decision-makers therefore have to make more efforts to justify decisions over military means. It also generates a stronger preference to use military force in a restrained way to minimise risks of casualties. A stronger normative attachment to power politics, i.e. the transatlantic relationship, makes British decision-makers less likely to refuse requests for military assistance from the US and lower domestic and international authorisation requirements make it easier for British decision-makers to resort to the use of military force. Although the introduction already suggested that Germany and the UK differ in the frequency and intensity with which they intervened abroad, this difference now needs to be demonstrated in more detail to render further plausibility to the claim that there is a positive correlation between strategic culture and behaviour.

4.1 German military interventions abroad since 1990

Although this book focuses on military interventions since 1990 it is necessary to take a brief glimpse at the period before 1990. Since the formative moment of German strategic culture in 1945, the *Stunde Null*, Germany did not deploy troops abroad except for disaster relief operations.[1] One might argue that this was due to the occupying powers imposing restraint upon Germany after its defeat. After all, it only regained full sovereignty with its reunification in 1990. However, instances in which Germany showed restraint even though its allies asked for military assistance speak against such explanations. In 1987 for example the US sought to secure the passage of oil tankers in the Persian Gulf, which led to clashes with Iranian forces. The US government asked its European allies for assistance. Germany was asked to send minesweepers and frigates to protect the oil tankers. The German government declined this request with reference to the constrictions of its Basic Law but sent a few ships to the Mediterranean so that US ships stationed there could be employed at the Persian Gulf.[2]

To test neorealist and moderately constructivist variables against each other it is more interesting to analyse Germany's behaviour after the end of the Cold War. For this reason this time period received abundant scholarly attention. The Gulf War 1990 to 1991 provided the first security and defence policy challenge for the newly reunified Germany. Already in August 1990 the US asked for German troops to be deployed to the Gulf.[3] After short contemplation the German government refused and, as usual, referred to the constraints of its Basic Law. Instead, Germany supported the US and its allies financially with 18 billion DM, almost 10 percent of all international expenditure on the war[4]. This suggests that German strategic culture, specifically norms generating preferenes for non-military means to resolve conflicts and to avoid exposure to risky combat situations, affected its behaviour towards the Gulf Crisis in 1990. As in 1987, norm categories one and two came to clash with the third category, Germany's strong attachment to multilateralism or, in this case, transatlanticism. This resulted in the compromise of financial assistance. As Hellmann argues: "All in all, the conviction or at least the hope prevailed in Germany that a peaceful, political solution to the conflict can be

[1] Deutsche Bundeswehr 2007a: „Abgeschlossene Einsätze", 18/09/07, www.einsatz.bundeswehr.de
[2] Hellmann 2005, p. 196; Baumann, Rainer 2001: "German Security Policy Within NATO", in: Rittberger, Volker (ed.): German Foreign Policy Since Unification, Manchester University Press, Manchester, p. 169
[3] Hellmann 2005, p. 196
[4] Hellmann 2005, p. 196; Longhurst 2004, pp. 57 – 59, 74; Kaiser, Karl/Becher, Klaus 1992: "Deutschland und der Irak Konflikt: Internationale Sicherheitsverantwortung Deutschlands und Europas nach der deutschen Vereinigung", *Arbeitspapiere zur Internationalen Politik* 68 (February), DGAP, Bonn, pp. 47 - 52

achieved with the help of diplomatic means and economic sanctions against Iraq. The thought that instead coercive means would probably be necessary was simply incompatible with German political culture, which assumed that conflicts can be resolved peacefully."[5]

From the Gulf War it became clear that core values such as alliance solidarity, humanitarian concerns and responsibility towards Israel will increasingly come to clash with stubborn antimilitarism. After the Gulf War Germany sent minesweepers to the Persian Gulf and assisted in relief efforts for Kurdish refugees between April and June 1991. These actions were justified on humanitarian grounds and notions of German 'responsibility'.[6] The Bundeswehr also participated in the UNTAC mission to Cambodia in May 1992 with around 140 paramedics, the UNOSOM II mission to Somalia with 1640 soldiers to provide logistical support, the UNAMIR mission to Rwanda with two aircraft and 30 air force soldiers for logistical support and the UNPROFOR mission to Bosnia and Herzegovina 1993 – 1995 with air force and engineering staff.[7] Participation in these missions signified readiness to deploy troops for humanitarian purposes but only for non-combative tasks.

Since 1992 Germany also participated in the NATO operation Sharp Guard to supervise the Adriatic embargo against the Federal Republic of Yugoslavia (Serbia) with one ship.[8] As this was a non-combative task within the NATO area. When asked to provide military personnel to participate in the AWACS reconnaissance mission Operation Deny Flight to control and enforce a no-fly zone over Bosnia the German government declined because the FDP considered such a combative mission as incompatible with Basic Law.[9] Heated debates ensued as the CDU argued this would severely damage Germany's credibility as a loyal NATO partner. The constitutional court eventually settled this 'out-of-area debate' in 1994. It decided that 'out-of-area' missions conformed to the constitution as long as the *Bundestag* approved. After this decision Germany eventually contributed military personnel and 14 Tornado aircraft to Operation Deny Flight.[10] In Germany it was constantly stressed that this was not a combative operation. The 'out-of-area' debate illustrates Germany's peculiar security policy behaviour. As Hellmann put it: "That also deployments, which were regarded as wholly unproblematic in many other NATO countries, led to controversial debates in Germany, is by itself already an indication of something like a political culture of military restraint exerting its influence."[11]

So far the frequency and intensity of German military interventions abroad seem to correlate with a strategic culture of the restraint use of force, a strong attachment to multilateralism and high authorisation requirements.

Although the constitutional court's decision put an end to the legalistic character of German debates over troop deployment it did not spark an abrupt end of the restraint style of German security policy. In November 1994 Germany refused to supply Tornado planes to help NATO protect the withdrawal of UNPROFOR peacekeepers and only gave in after its allies applied pressure, stressing that it will not commit ground troops and justified this on grounds of alliance solidarity.[12] When the NATO-led IFOR mission took over from UNPROFOR in Bosnia in 1995 Germany participated with 3000 ground troops but the German contingent rather

---

[5] Translation by the author, original in German. Hellmann 2005, p. 196

[6] Longhurst 2004, p. 58

[7] Longhurst 2004, pp. 59 – 60, Hellmann 2005, p. 197

[8] Ibid., NATO 2003a: "Regional Headquarters Allied Forces Southern Europe Fact Sheet Operation Sharp Guard", 18/08/03, www.afsouth.nato.int/operations/SharpGuard/SharpGuardFactSheet.htm,

[9] Longhurst, p. 60 – 64

[10] NATO 2003b: "Regional Headquarters Allied Forces Southern Europe Fact Sheet Operation Deny Flight", 18/07/03, www.afsouth.nato.int/operations/denyflight/DenyFlightFactSheet.htm

[11] Translation by the author, original in German: „Das es auch bei Einsätzen, die in vielen anderen NATO-Ländern als völlig unproblematisch angesehen wurden, in Deutschland zu kontroversen Debatten kam, ist für sich gesehen bereits ein Zeichen dafür, dass hier so etwas wie die politische Kultur der militärischen Zurückhaltung ihren Einfluss übte". Hellmann 2005, p. 198

[12] Longhurst 2004, p. 65

acted as part of NATO's back-up support.[13] It was stationed outside Bosnia and was significantly smaller than the British and largely consisted of paramedics and supply troops to support the French contingent.[14]

In December 1996, when IFOR turned into SFOR to secure the Dayton agreement that ended the Bosnian war Germany participated with 1700 troops stationed inside Bosnia as an 'equal partner'.[15] This represented the first step away from Germany's strictly restrained security policy. German participation in the Kosovo War 1999 represented the second.

Despite the absence of a UN mandate Bundeswehr participated in Operation Allied Force with 14 Tornado jets and air force soldiers for the reconnaissance and combat of enemy air defence systems.[16] Although small in size this deployment signified Germany's first combat mission since the Bundeswehr's creation. After the cessation of air strikes the Bundestag agreed to send up to 8000 soldiers into Kosovo as part of NATO's KFOR mission to implement UN Security Council resolution 1244.[17] These developments highlight profound changes in Germany's security policy behaviour since 1990. However, sings of a restrained style of security policy are still visible. Germany was always firmly against the use of ground troops[18] and continued intensive diplomatic efforts after the start of the bombing campaign to avert military action or at least garner international legitimacy for the campaign. Foreign Minister Joschka Fischer's peace plan also sought to bring on board Russia and China into the peace process and to stabilise the region through socio-economic measures.[19] These developments suggest an increasing readiness by German decision-makers to use military force for humanitarian purposes. However, one could still argue that effects of Germany's strategic culture are discernible, especially a preference for non-military means and for using force in a restraint way as well as a commitment to multilateralism. Though they participated German elites were uneasy about authorising the coercive use of force without UN approval.

In the aftermath of the terrorist attacks of 11 September 2001 (9/11) a number of further challenges confronted German security policy. Although Germany did not participate in the US-led invasion of Afghanistan it hosted the Petersberg Conference after the invasion and deployed around 1000 troops to the international protection force ISAF in Afghanistan, which gradually increased to 3155 troops mainly based in the country's north. On 7 November 2001 the Bundestag also decided to participate in the fight against terrorism through Operation Enduring Freedom (OEF) with a maximum of 3900 soldiers, most of which were marines deployed to the Horn of Africa but also defensive forces for NBC weapons deployed to Kuwait to protect civilians and American troops stationed there from possible Iraqi attacks.[20]

Apart from these missions responsive to 11 September Germany contributed to several other international military operations. The largest were 600 troops deployed to the 30 days long "Operation Essential Harvest" to disarm ethnic Albanian groups and destroy their weapons in the Former Yugoslav Republic of Macedonia and 780 troops to the EU-led EUFOR Mission to the Democratic Republic of Congo to ensure peace and stability during parliamentary elections.[21]

---

[13] Ibid, p. 66; Hellmann 2005, p. 202

[14] Hellmann 2005, p. 198

[15] Longhurst 2004, p. 66; Bundeswehr 2007b: „Chronologie der Einsätze der Bundeswehr in Bosnien-Herzegowina", 5/12/07, www.einsatz.bundeswehr.de

[16] Longhurst 2004, p. 71; Hyde-Price 2001, p. 19 (Longhurst and Hyde-Price write of only four German Tornado jets); Deutscher Bundestag 1999: Plenary Protocol 14/34, 21/04/1999, http://dip.bundestag.de/btp/14/14034.asc

[17] Bundeswehr 2007b, http://www.einsatz.bundeswehr.de

[18] Hyde-Price, Adrian 1999: "Berlin Republic Takes to Arms", *The World Today,* June; Von Ilsemann, Siegesmund 1999: „Fertiger Plan für den Bodenkrieg", *Der Spiegel* 17/1999; Cohen 1999

[19] Longhurst 2004, pp. 69 – 72

[20] Hellmann 2005, p. 200 – 201

[21] Bundeswehr 2007b, www.einsatz.bundeswehr.de

From this short review of Bundeswehr operations since 1990 one can draw two conclusions. On the one hand one can observe a sharp increase in the frequency and intensity of German military interventions abroad, which shows that German decision-makers became significantly less disinclined to authorise the use of force. On the other hand one can discern traits of security policy in line with those suggested by an analysis of German strategic culture. These are a preference for the containment and limitation of the use of force, even in cases when Germany was willing to use force in principle, and a proclivity to act together with partners as far as possible or a normative attachment to multilateralism.[22]

[22] Hellmann 2005, p. 200

4.2 British military interventions abroad since 1990

Neeedless to say that unlinke Germany, the UK fought a number of small- to medium-scale wars between 1945 and 1990. The Suez Crisis 1956 -57 and the Falklands War 1982 are probably the most prominent of these whereas operations to defeat insurgencies, such as in Malaya 1948 – 1960 or in Kenya 1952 -1956 are less well known today. The UK also sent minesweepers to the Gulf in 1987 – 88.[23]

It is rather difficult to extract from the literature when exactly how many British troops were deployed where to do what since 1990. This in itself is telling. German troop deployments since the Cold War are vastly covered by the literature because they are more of a sensation. British troop deployments on the other hand seem more like a routine and a matter of course. Yielding a strong response to the Iraqi invasion of Kuwait, the UK deployed some 46000 troops to the Gulf War in 1991, 47 of which suffered casualties and 15 were held prisoners of war. From 1991 to 2003 The Royal Air Force patrolled no-fly-zones established over Iraq to protect Kurdish and Shiite minorities.[24] These resulted from an initiative by the Major government, "which in turn helped to set one of the most important precedents of the post-Cold War period, that of humanitarian intervention in the affairs of sovereign states".[25] The UK participated widely in international peacekeeping operations. In 1993 alone 4000 British personnel took part in six operations.[26] As of November 1994 the UK provided 3405 troops and 19 military observers to UNPROFOR.[27] When NATO took over command in Bosnia and turned UNPROFOR into IFOR Britain committed 13000 troops[28] and served as a framework nation for the Multinational Division South-West, with France and the US taking over the command over the other two sectors of Bosnia.[29] The last remaining 700 British SFOR troops left Bosnia in March 2007 due to the improved security situation there.[30] Although the UK was in no position to put an end to atrocities in Bosnia until the US decided to intervene it did "far more than most", as former Prime Minister John Major put it in his autobiography.[31] Its commitment indicates a relatively proactive and internationalist style of security policy assigning a relatively high preference rank to the steadfast use of force for humanitarian purposes, which correlates with the findings in the previous chapter. The Bosnian War did not provide for easy options if one did not want to stand by its televised horrors. The UK seems to have opted for a middle way between full-scale invasion and by-standing, which achieved unsatisfactory results. Then Foreign Secretary Douglas Hurd subsequently wrote that "if firm and rapid reaction would have stopped the crisis we would have agreed. Casualties would have been accepted if a quick and favourable outcome could have been assured."[32] This, again, correlates with assertions about the effects of British strategic culture made previously.

Britain played the most important role after the US in Operation Allied Force. It provided 48 out of 829 aircraft, including important air-to-air refuelling systems. After the air campaign it provided around 10500 troops to KFOR, including its first commander, General

---

[23] Mangold 2001, p. 154

[24] Ibid, p. 115

[25] Ibid, p. 151; see also Munro, Sir Alan 1996: "An Arabian Affair", Brasseys, London, p. 59; Major, John 1999: "The Autobiography", HarperCollins, London, p. 536

[26] Ibid, p. 96

[27] UN Department of Public Information 1996: "United Nations Protection Force", 09/1996, http://www.un.org/Depts/dpko/dpko/co_mission/unprof_b.htm

[28] US Department of Defense Technical Information Center 1995: "Operation Joint Endeavour Fact Sheet", 11/12/95, http://www.dtic.mil/bosnia/fs/fs006b.html

[29] Hellmann 2005, p. 198; Wentz, Larry 1997: "Lessons from Bosnia: The IFOR Experience", Department of Defense Command and Control Research Program, Washington D.C., p. 36

[30] BBC 2007: "Where are British Troops and Why?", 02/10/07 http://news.bbc.co.uk/2/hi/uk_news/4094818.stm

[31] Major 1999, p. 548; quoted in Mangold 2001, p. 152

[32] Hurd, Douglas 1997: "The Search for Peace", Little, Brown, London, p. 130; quoted in Mangold 2001, p. 152

Michael Jackson.[33] Apart from Labour, the Liberal Democrats and the Conservatives endorsed the NATO campaign although contention emerged about the legal basis of the air strikes and the fact that after sixty days into the bombing campaign there has been no substantive vote in parliament authorising it,[34] a fact which correlates with previous findings on norms concerning domestic authorisation requirements.

In late August 2001 Britain led "Operation Essential Harvest" to disarm rivalling factions in Macedonia, contributed around 1500 of the total 3500 troops and suffered one casualty.[35]

The UK's military involvement in Sierra Leone in 2000 played a crucial role in ending the horrific civil war that raged since 1991. Operation Palliser involved the deployment of around 1300 troops in May 2000 originally with the goal of evacuating British citizens but which extended the mission to gain control over the capital Freetown and assist the deployment of further UN peacekeepers for the UNAMSIL mission. After the situation in Sierra Leone stabilised in mid-June the UK left behind around 200 troops to train Sierra Leone's army. On 10 September eleven British soldiers were taken hostage by a group called the "West Side Boys". The UK Special Forces SAS then spearheaded the rescue mission Operation Barras, whose success arguably represented a major turning point in the civil war.[36] Due to the challenging nature of this operation participating forces nicknamed it "Operation Certain Death".[37] In October the UK strengthened its commitment again to 650 personnel to bolster UNAMSIL.[38] This mission highlights a high risk tolerance and a strong commitment to the use of force for humanitarian purposes.

In Afghanistan the UK was involved from the first day of attacks in October 2001 with its Royal Navy and Royal Air Force (RAF). From November 2001 to July 2002 the UK assigned over 4000 troops to the US-led OEF operations,[39] including a battle group of 1700 soldiers to fight Al Qaeda and the Taliban on the ground.[40] After the fall of the Taliban the British contribution to ISAF gradually increased to 7753 troops, which makes it the second largest troop contributor, to the country's troublesome southern Helmand province.[41]

The UK used military force against Iraq already a number of times before its most prominent recent deployment. In 1998 for instance "Operation Desert Fox" consisted of 250 bombing missions against Iraqi WMD facilities.[42] During the Iraq War 2003 Britain was the only state other than the US that committed "more than a token force".[43] Its commitment peaked with 46,000 troops in March and April 2003. The toll of British fatalities is at 174 as of 17 December 2007.[44] Although the decision to participate in the Iraq War was heavily contested domestically the previous chapter suggests that British strategic culture, particularly the elites' normative attachment to Atlanticism as well as norms regarding justified goals for and preferred modes of the use of force, was a necessary condition for such large-scale employment of military force.

---

[33] Williams, Paul D. 2005: "British Foreign Policy under New Labour", Palgrave Macmillan, New York, p. 64

[34] Williams 2005, p. 65; House of Commons 1999: Debates, *Hansard*, 18/05/1999, column 923

[35] Ibid, p. 129; "British Soldier Killed in Macedonia", *BBC News*, 27/08/01, 31/01/08 http://news.bbc.co.uk/2/hi/uk_news/1511418.stm

[36] Williams 2005, pp. 83 – 84

[37] Lewis, Damien 2005: "Operation Certain Death", Century, London.

[38] Williams 2005, pp. 83 – 84

[39] Ibid, p. 50

[40] British Ministry of Defence 2007a: "Operations in Afghanistan: Background Briefing 1", 10/10/07, 31/01/08, www.mod.uk/DefenceInternet/FactSheets/OperationsFactsheets/OperationsInAfghanistanBackgroundBriefing1

[41] NATO 2007: "ISAF", 05/12/2007, http://www.nato.int/isaf/docu/epub/pdf/isaf_placemat.pdf

[42] Royal Air Force 2008: "Chapter 6: Return to Expeditionary Warfare", p. 289, www.raf.mod.uk

[43] Murray, Williamson/Scales, Robert 2003: "The War in Iraq", Harvard University Press, Cambridge MA, p. 123; quoted in Williams 2005, p. 185

[44] British Ministry of Defence 2007b: "Operations in Iraq: Facts and Figures", 17/12/07, http://www.mod.uk/DefenceInternet/FactSheets/OperationsFactsheets/OperationsInIraqFactsandFigures.htm

4.3 Summarising and synthesising the findings

From this survey of British and German military interventions abroad since 1990 it becomes apparent that the UK used military force more frequently and more intensively than Germany since 1990 and that the effects of differences in all four norm categories of British and German strategic cultures are discernible in their record of the use of military force since 1990. British foreign, security and defence policy behaviour is marked by internationalism and what former British Defence Secretary Geoffrey Hoon termed a "no-nonsense pragmatism"[45]: it is driven by humanitarian concerns at least as much as expediency. This is not to say that the UK is a bellicose nation but that British strategic culture, in particular a higher acceptance of casualties and a higher proclivity to deem the use of force justified, places military force on a higher position in preference rankings compared to German strategic culture. Germany displayed the behaviour of a civilian power: it went to war less frequently, showed more restraint in the use of force when at war, placed heavy emphasis on very close cooperation with allies and partners and heatedly debated decisions to go to war before deployment. Although one can observe a dramatic increase in the number and intensity of German military deployments they still remain on a lower level than the UK's. The previous chapter suggested that German strategic culture may have changed since 1990 but that there are still significant differences to the UK's strategic culture. This all suggests that there is a positive correlation between strategic culture and behaviour as regards the use of military force both across cases and across time within the case of Germany, which substantiates the second hypothesis of this book.

The table below shows a summary of all military interventions abroad of which there was information available. However, especially information on British operations has to be treated with care, as it is difficult to find reliable and complete information regarding troop numbers and missions. Some operations may have been omitted and troop numbers may be inaccurate. Deployments are colour-coded into different shades of grey according to the perceived intensity with which force was to be used in each mission, with pale-grey for low intensity operations, grey for lower medium, dark-grey for upper medium and black for highly intensive operations.

Table 13: British and German military operations abroad since 1990

Germany		UK	
Mission	Contribution	Mission	Contribution
UNAMIC/UNTAC (Cambodia 1991 – 93)	Up to 140 paramedics for medical support	Operation Desert Storm (Iraq 1990 - 91)	Up to 46,000 combat troops to force Iraqi troops to withdraw from Kuwait
UNSCOM (Iraq 1991 – 96)	37 troops to provide logistical support	Operation Provide Comfort (Northern Iraq April – June 91)	Around 3300 troops delivering humanitarian aid and security to Kurdish refugees[46]
UNOSOM II (Somalia 1993 – 94)	1640 troops for logistical support of UN troops	Operation Warden (Iraq 1991 – 2003)	Royal Air Force patrolling northern no-fly-zone to protect Kurdish minority[47]

[45] Hoon, Geoffrey 2000: "Kosovo: One Year After", *Journal of the Royal United Services Institute* (April), p. 5
[46] Royal Air Force 2008, p. 287
[47] Royal Air Force 2008, pp. 287 – 289

UNOMIG (Georgia 1994 – present)	3 unarmed military observers and 9 medics	Operation Jural (Iraq 1992 – 98)	Royal Air Force patrolling northern no-fly-zone to protect Shiite minority[48]
UNAMIR (Rwanda July – December 1994)	30 air force soldiers providing logistical support	UNAMIR (Rwanda July – December 1994)	225 troops and medics for medical assistance and mass grave location
		UNAVEM III (Angola 1995)	650 troops for logistical support and 70 infantry for protection.[49]
UNPROFOR (Bosnia 1993 – 95)	Logistical support	UNPROFOR (Bosnia 1993 – 95)	3405 troops to ensure demilitarisation of designated areas and aid delivery
IFOR (Bosnia 1995 – 96)	3000 support troops stationed in Croatia	IFOR (Bosnia 1995 – 96)	13,000 troops to implement peace agreement
SFOR (1996 – 2004, since then EUFOR)	Around 3000 troops, including combat units	SFOR (1996 – 2007)	13,000 to 700 troops to ensure upholding of peace agreement
		Operation Desert Fox (Iraq 1998)	Royal Air Force flying 250 bombing missions against Iraqi targets
Operation Allied Force (Kosovo 1999)	14 Tornado jets, around 500 sorties to halt ethnic cleansing	Operation Allied Force (Kosovo 1999)	48 aircraft and 1618 sorties to halt ethnic cleansing
KFOR (Kosovo, since 1999)	Around 5800 combat troops to implement peace in Kosovo	KFOR (Kosovo, since 1999)	10500 combat troops to implement peace in Kosovo
INTERFET (East Timor 1999 – 2000)	Around 100 troops to provide medical support	INTERFET (East Timor 1999 – 2000	Around 270 troops for peacekeeping[50]
Operation Essential Harvest (Macedonia 2001)	600 soldiers for disarmament	Operation Essential Harvest (Macedonia 2001)	1500 soldiers for disarmament
Operation Enduring Freedom (Mostly Horn of Africa and Kuwait, 2002 – present)	Up to 3900 soldiers (currently between 240 and 450) stationed to monitoring shipping routes and in case of Iraqi attack with WMD	Operation Enduring Freedom (Mostly Afghanistan, 2001 – present)	Over 4000 troops to fight Taliban and Al Qaeda forces in Afghanistan

[48] Ibid.

[49] Bellamy, Christopher 1995: "UK Forces Angola-bound" *The Independent* 14/04/95

[50] Information on INTERFET derived from: Paul, James/Spirit, Martin 2002: "Riots, Rebellions, Gun Boats and Peacekeepers", 2002, 31/01/08, http://www.britains-smallwars.com/RRGP/EastTimor.html

ISAF (Afghanistan 2001 – present)	Up to 3500 troops for peacebuilding and provincial reconstruction	ISAF (Afghanistan 2001 – present)	Up to 7753 troops for peacebuilding and provincial reconstruction
EUFOR DR Congo (DR Congo July – November 2006)	780 troops to ensure smooth running of parliamentary elections	Operations Palliser and Barras (Sierra Leone 2000)	1300 troops to evacuate British citizens and enforce peace in Sierra Leone
UNIFIL (Lebanon 2006 – present)	Up to 2400 marines patrolling the Lebanese coast to prevent arms smuggling[51]	Operation ARTEMIS (DR Congo	88 engineers to provide technical assistance to French-led EU force[52]
		Operation Iraqi Freedom (Iraq 2002 – present)	Up to 46,000 troops to invade and occupy Iraq

When measuring frequency through a simple mission count the difference is rather slim. Yet this value is rather meaningless since there is a high possibility of omitted deployments due to lack of available information and it is necessary to distinguish between size and mandate of the operation as it would be rather nonsensical to compare the deployment of three military observers and ten medics to Georgia with that of 46,000 combat units to Iraq. When counting only combat missions one can count twelve British and six German such missions. A more meaningful value for the difference in frequency of the use of force is a combined mission and head count, which would contrast 24,137 German with 136,816 British soldiers deployed since 1990. This approximate figure has to be treated with care but it illustrates that there is a vast difference in the intensity and frequency with which force is used. After all, the UK deployed more troops in the Gulf War than Germany altogether since 1990.

[51] Bundeswehr 2007a, www.einsatz.bundeswehr.de

[52] House of Commons 2003: Debates, *Hansard* Column 697W, 08/07/03, http://www.parliament.the-stationery-office.com/pa/cm200203/cmhansrd/vo030708/text/30708w09.htm

5.) Instances of intervention

To move beyond establishing a correlation by demonstrating that there are causal links between strategic culture and behaviour it is necessary to analyse individual instances in which the two countries decided to employ military force. The introduction stated that norms generate collective expectations, which shape actor's preferences, thus determine which options are considered and which are not. This chapter will attempt to trace this causal process from norms to collective expectations and actors' preferences to behaviour in the use of military force as far as time, space and accessibility of information allow, in four cases of military intervention. Special emphasis will be placed on how decisions to go to war were debated. Preference rankings can be discerned through a qualitative analysis of how the use of force was justified in these crucial debates. If there is a systematic difference across and recurrence within cases in patterns of justifications for the use of force this indicates that two distinct strategic cultures affect differing behaviour. But also the quantitative dimension of these debates, the time and effort spent by politico-military elites on justifying the use of military force before a decision was made, indicates preferences derived from strategic culture. This is particularly the case when a specific decision deviates from strategic culture or the options posed by a specific situation matches strategic preferences in some communities more than others. Apart from crucial debates referents of strategic culture can also be found in instances in which original strategic decisions are subject to review once an operation is underway. It will therefore be tested whether strategic culture then still limits the options considered.

Chapter 4 already suggested that the Gulf War 1990 represents a case in which the effects of German and British strategic cultures in the early 1990s were detectable. However, since case selection for this book already took place on the dependent variable it would not be very constructive to select a rather soft case in which Germany did not to use military force at all but the UK did so quite intensively at a time when neorealist predictions about the future of reunited Germany's security policy were yet to be made. Operation Allied Force (OAF) on the other hand represents a hard case in which Germany used force without UN Security Council approval and while it was governed by a red-green coalition. Military involvement in Afghanistan since 2001 also represents a recent hard case since there are no structural reasons for differences in behaviour in response to 9/11. Apart from these two hard cases the book will also compare and contrast two separate but comparable military interventions which are particularly well suited to point out differences in strategic culture and their effect on behaviour. These are the UK's military involvement in Sierra Leone in 2000 and Germany's involvement in the Democratic Republic of Congo in 2006.

5.1 Operation Allied Force 1999

5.1.1 The British decision to participate in OAF

While the humanitarian crisis in the Serbian province of Kosovo lingered on in the summer of 1998 the international society in the form of the Contact Group of six states[1], debated how it should react.

The first head of government who moved beyond saying that 'all options were being considered' and brought up the option of military force was Tony Blair.[2] In a question and answer session on engagements in the House of Commons on 3 June 1998 Liberal Democrats leader Mr Paddy Ashdown asked:

> "Does the Prime Minister agree that, one, the efforts of the international community so far to persuade President Milosevic to exercise some restraint in Kosovo have had no visible effect; two, that the situation in the province is now speedily deteriorating; and, three, that in these matters it is far, far better to take strong, preventive action early than to wait until one is left with doing too little, too late?"[3]

The Prime Minister replied: "I agree with that." Furthermore: "I want to make it very clear that we are watching the situation in Kosovo extremely carefully. We believe that we cannot afford to have an extension of violence and disorder there." Referring to NATO action in Bosnia in 1995 he continued:

> "Before, in a similar situation nearby, the international community acted with great firmness, and we must make sure that we do the same again. In answer to the question from the Opposition Benches, 'Why bother?' we bother because disorder in that part of the world would have a huge impact on all of us, including this country."[4]

Mr Ashdown, in return, reminded the Prime Minister "that it was during the previous United Kingdom presidency in 1992 that we missed the decisive opportunity to act early in Bosnia". He further asked the Prime Minister about the specific actions he envisages and whether these include "to make it absolutely clear to President Milosevic that if he should act in gross contravention of international human rights and with the effect of destabilising the nations in the area, the international community will regard that as an act in violation of international law". Blair replied:

> "In respect of the specific action that we will take, I have already said, and will repeat, that we do not believe that we could afford to have disorder spreading in that part of the world. I hope that that is a sufficiently clear message to Mr. Milosevic. (…) Again, I make it clear that we do not believe that it could be in the interests of our country or of the world community to allow a similar situation to develop there as developed in Bosnia."[5]

These answers represent a clear warning to Milosevic that NATO would not tolerate an intensification of the conflict in Kosovo, thus introduce the option to use military force. They are representative of several traits of New Labour's stance on the use of military force. Firstly, the reference to the "huge impact on all of us" highlights two main driving forces behind British foreign policy since 1990: humanitarian concerns and expediency. As the British ambassador to the UK Sir Alan Munro commented on the British response to the invasion of Kuwait

---

[1] They were: United States, Russia, UK, France, Germany and Italy, which joined in 1995. The Contact Group was formed, in part by the UK, at the beginning of the Bosnian war to provide a central body for international peace efforts. See Bellamy, Alex J. 2002: "Kosovo and International Society", Palgrave MacMillan, Basingstoke, p. 223

[2] Ibid, p. 86

[3] House of Commons 1998: Debates, *Hansard*, 3 June 1998, Column 360, http://www.publications.parliament.uk/pa/cm199798/cmhansrd/vo980603/debtext/80603-23.htm#80603-23_spmin0

[4] Ibid.

[5] Ibid, Column 360

1990: "Moral arguments carried just as much weight as those derived from expediency."[6] Under New Labour, the balance may have tilted towards the former.

Secondly, the frequent references to Bosnia indicate that events surrounding this war helped in the formation of a firm belief in the decisive use of force as an effective means to pursue the recurring security and defence goal of halting atrocities where they happen, especially when they happen nearby.

Lastly and most importantly an effect of strategic culture is discernible in the time at which Blair gave these answers, namely before any other head of government in the contact group issued such warnings. This indicates that the UK is a community with a strategic culture that places the use of force as a means to pursue the UK's security and defence goals on a relatively high position in preference rankings. This is in correlation with the fact that, as will be elaborated later, the UK's and Germany's behaviour differ drastically in that decisions to use force were often made by initiative in the UK and in response to pronouncements of allies and partners in Germany. All in all, the Blair government's early engagement in the Kosovo tragedy highlights its internationalist, proactive security strategy representative of a country that is very alert of events worldwide and does not shy away from formulating firm responses to these events.

The way the decision to use force against Serbia formed within the Blair government is indicative of a strategic culture providing the necessary condition for this decision to come about. There are several indications that the impulse originated from Blair, "who as leader of the opposition had strongly criticised John Major's handling of the Bosnian war and was determined not to make the same mistakes as his predecessor".[7] When he consulted his government on the action it should take towards Kosovo he allegedly stated that "the only question that matters is whether you are prepared to use force. And we have to be. Reports indicate a level of butchery that risks escalating into another Bosnia".[8] The strength of his conviction and the autonomy with which he could act are also revealed by the fact that while his government insisted that any action would have to be taken multilaterally Downing Street asked the Ministry of Defence to investigate options for acting unilaterally as early as June 1998, according to the British journalist John Kampfner and the Australian political scientist Alex Bellamy.[9] One scenario envisaged the deployment of up to 60.000 British soldiers as "heavy peacekeepers".[10] And already in June 1998 some senior members of the government believed a ground intervention would be necessary. On 5 June 1998, while the US administration was still torn between 'activist' and 'reluctant' camps over the Kosovo crisis[11] the British government drafted a Security Council resolution invoking chapter VII by authorising 'all necessary means' to stabilise the situation. Explaining this proposal a British official who asked not to be named explained the *Washington Post* that "there has been a hardening of the mood in London, from the top down. ... The only thing that would change Milosevic's actions would be [military] actions in and over Kosovo itself." He further stated that Foreign Secretary Robin Cook discussed the idea of a tougher approach with US Secretary of State Madeleine K. Albright and that London was also asking NATO's Secretary General Javier Solana, "with a good deal of urgency", to examine various military options.[12] By this time the US did "not have a government position yet" towards Kosovo but since the British draft resolution it was "evolving pretty rapidly", a senior US official said to the newspaper. He added: "I think we

---

[6] Munro, Sir Alan 1996: "An Arabian Affair", Brasseys, London, p. 59; quoted in Mangold 2001, p. 151
[7] Bellamy 2002, p. 87
[8] Bellamy 2002, p. 87 (He obtained this information through a private email from a source in Whitehall)
[9] Ibid; Kampfner, John 2003: "Blair's Wars", Simon & Schuster, London, p. 49.
[10] Kampfner 2003, p. 49; Guthrie, General Sir Charles 200, "Bringing the Armed Forces into a New Millenium", *Royal Defence Institute Journal* (February), p. 3.
[11] Smith, R. Jeffrey 1998: "Officials Seek Kosovo Intervention, British Draft of U.N. Resolution Urges 'All Necessary Measures'", *Washington Post*, 6 June 1998
[12] Ibid, also quoted in Bellamy 2002, p. 87

are going to favour this."[13] It seems as if the British government contributed significantly to the 'activist' camp eventually winning over the 'reluctant' camp in the debate over the Kosovo tragedy within the US administration. On 11 June 1998 at a summit of NATO defence ministers British Defence Secretary George Robertson stated that a NATO-intervention would be a question of days, not of weeks.[14] This determined, early and proactive British reaction to events in Kosovo highlights that British strategic culture allows for decision-makers to place the use of force relatively high in ranked sets of security policy options.

A proactive style of security policy is discernible in the dynamism emanating from the Blair government in efforts to rally international support for military action. After drafting the resolution the UK brought up the option of military force at meetings of the European Union, NATO and the Contact Group.[15] Together with the US, it launched "a sustained and multi-faceted diplomatic offensive throughout the summer and early autumn of 1998" to secure agreement among NATO allies.[16] Yet these efforts initially only met with little response. Amongst NATO allies, there was no support at all for a ground invasion and several reservations about the idea of air strikes. Allies questioned their ability to achieve NATO's desired goals and highlighted the threat to air crew posed by Serbia's air defence system. France and Germany insisted on UN Security Council authorisation although there was no reasonable chance to obtain this in the light of Chinese and Russian opposition. A crucial turning point came on 6 October 1998 at a meeting of the foreign ministers of the Contact Group in a side room at Heathrow Airport, which basically concluded debates on the use of force within the group. Notably, the Russian foreign minister Igor Ivanov implied that Russia would use its veto in the Security Council on any resolution authorising NATO to use force against Serbia but if NATO went ahead nonetheless it would "just make a lot of noise"[17]. This tacit assurance that Russia would not take military action gave significant impetus to agreement on NATO action against Yugoslavia even without UN Security Council approval.

By September 1998 joint U.S. and UK efforts to introduce the idea of air strikes to the international community had paid out: most NATO allies had become generally, if uneasily, supportive of the idea, although they rejected a ground invasion.[18] In mid-June, the US was the first to join in with the UK over its fears of 'another Bosnia'. Others, including Germany, needed more persuasion but eventually joined in, too. Eventually, on 23 September 1998 NATO issued an Activation Warning for a phased air campaign in Kosovo. It is telling that one could reasonably argue that NATO action in Kosovo was more or less Blair's work. The crucial debate in the UK over events in Kosovo in 1998 reveals that state preferences, the main empirical referent of a strategic culture according to Johnston, favoured the decisive use of military force.

With the credible threat of air strikes at hand the international community and US diplomat Richard Holbrooke in particular applied diplomatic pressure on Milosevic, who then complied and managed to fend off air strikes until the international community saw the urgent need for action once again by spring 1999. After the exhaustion of an observer mission, a peace conference and final talks between Milosevic and Holbrooke NATO decided to launch Operation Allied Force on 24 March 1999. On the day before in the afternoon the Prime Minister made his final remarks on the impending military action in the House of Commons. This debate reaffirms many of the points made previously about the discernible effects of British strategic

---

[13] Smith 1998

[14] Krause, Joachim 2000: "Deutschland und die Kosovo-Krise", in: Reuter, Jens/Clewing, Conrad (ed.) 2000: "Der Kosovo Konflikt. Ursachen, Verlauf, Perspektiven", Wieser Verlag, Klagenfurt, p. 403.

[15] Ibid.

[16] Bellamy 2002, p. 87

[17] Richard Holbrooke quoting Ivanov in his account of the Heathrow Airport meeting, Judah, Tim 2000: "Kosovo: War and Revenge", Yale University Press, New Haven and London, p. 183; also quoted in Bellamy 2002, p. 93

[18] Bellamy 2002, p. 89

culture that provided the necessary condition for Britain's behaviour as regards the use of military force against Serbia in 1999.
The parliamentary session was marked by consent between Labour, Liberal Democrats as and Conservatives on the legitimacy and necessity of the attacks as well as awareness of their risky nature. After Blair's opening remarks the leader of the Conservative opposition, William Hague, first and foremost expressed "the Opposition's wholehearted support for the British forces who might have to take part in the NATO action, for the service men and women who will be backing up those front-line forces, and for the families of those who might have to risk their lives as they do their jobs."[19] And the leader of the Liberal Democrats, Menzies Campbell, concurred that "None of us should underestimate the risk of casualties on either side. If air strikes prove to be necessary, those who advocate them and those who support them – as I do – might have to live with some extremely painful consequences."[20]
Notably, points of criticism were raised against Blair but more on grounds that he was doing too little and being too cautious with the use of force. When Labour MP Donald Anderson asked Blair whether there are circumstances in which he would be prepared to commit ground troops he answered that "I think that everyone shares a sense of reluctance to commit our forces. However, as my hon. Friend acknowledged that reluctance is overcome if circumstances dictate that it must be."[21] And the Conservative MP Sir Peter Tapsell commented:

> "Is it not almost certain that air strikes alone will not achieve NATO's objectives…? … Does the right hon. Gentleman realise that saying weasel words to the British people at this point is wrong because the Government are proposing to make war on Serbia…? If we are to pursue that policy, the British people should be told now that we are embarking inevitably on ground operations that will involve heavy casualties."[22]

The points and criticisms raised in this debate highlight the high risk tolerance and the relatively high position that British strategic culture assigns to the use of force as an option to achieve its security and defence goals. The use of force was justified with a great deal of humanitarianism and some expediency. This justification met the consent of a large majority in the House of Commons.
By the time the bombing campaign began virtually everyone in the British government and probably even Milosevic himself thought it would last no longer than 72 hours.[23] As it went on to last significantly longer criticism in the House of Commons grew louder, especially from Labour MPs such as Tony Benn, Iain Gallagan and Tam Dalyell. Points of contention were the lack of a UN mandate as the legal basis of NATO action and the high altitude from which NATO conducted the campaign, resulting in collateral damages. A particularly interesting point of contention was raised by Labour MP Jeremy Corbyn, who pointed out that … 60 days into the bombardment, there has been no substantive vote in the British Parliament on the authority of the Government to proceed with the bombardment of Yugoslavia. There has been no vote on whether there is to be a declaration of war, nor on the appropriation of vast amounts of money for this programme and there will not be a substantive vote either today, or, I suspect, on any other day."[24] The British Prime Minister enjoys this degree of autonomy in decisions to go to war because they fall under the Royal Prerogative. But this book argues that the Royal Prerogative, similar to the UK's nuclear weapons and aircraft carriers, exists because strategic culture provides the necessary condition.

---

[19] House of Commons 1999: Debates, *Hansard*, 23/03/99Column 163, http://www.publications.parliament.uk/pa/cm199899/cmhansrd/vo990323/debtext/90323-06.htm#90323-06_head0
[20] Ibid.
[21] Ibid, column 166
[22] Ibid, column 167
[23] Kampfner 2003, p. 44; Judah 2000, p. 228
[24] House of Commons 1999: Debates, *Hansard*, , 18/05/99, Column 923, http://www.publications.parliament.uk/pa/cm199899/cmhansrd/vo990518/debtext/90518-20.htm#90518-20_spnew; Williams 2005, p. 65;

5.1.1.1 Revising OAF in the UK

An indication of British strategic culture can be found in the preferences that form when the original strategy is under review during its implementation. As the Blair government considered the use of ground troops already in the summer of 1998, but dropped these plans in part because it could not win international support for them, one would expect that this option was brought up again once it became clear that the bombing campaign did not achieve the desired effects as early as originally hoped for. An indication of a strong preference for the use of ground troops, especially as the war went on, can be found in the support of several MPs from all parties in the House of Commons, as well as the Blair government's strong efforts to persuade the Clinton administration and other NATO allies of the need for ground troops. On 20 April in an Oral Question and Answer session in the House of Commons several MPs from the Labour and Liberal Democrat Parties asked Foreign Minister Robin Cook on the use of ground troops, implying in their questions their support for this option. Thus, Labour MP Oona King asked Cook:

> "A constituent of mine, Fadil Dugolli, visited me on Friday. He is a Kosovan refugee. His mother has died since the conflict began, and his two sisters are currently unaccounted for in Albania. He said to me, "Tell them not to stop the bombing. Milosevic has been killing us--murdering us--slowly, for years." Does my right hon. Friend agree with those words? Does my right hon. Friend agree that, if we want a United Nations protectorate and self-determination for the Kosovans, we must be determined to use ground troops?"[25]

And the Liberal Democrat MP Menzies Campbell asked Cook:

> "Today, in Brussels, the Prime Minister said that the Government intend to see the matter through to the end. Does the use of such an expression not imply that, if the option of using ground troops arises, NATO will be willing to impose its will on Kosovo and will not rely on receiving the agreement of Mr. Milosevic before determining to put troops into Kosovo?"[26]

Cook did not explicitly endorse this option. He answered that

> "We are willing to provide the ground troops to secure a ceasefire. We are also willing to put in ground troops at the point at which there may be no organised armed resistance, but an armed invasion would incur far greater casualties on both sides than the present military campaign."[27]

A day after, on 21 April, the leader of the Conservatives, William Hague, asked Blair on the issue of ground troops in the House of Commons, implying his support for this option in the question by saying that "There is widespread agreement throughout the House that, now that we have embarked on the action in Kosovo, it must succeed."[28] Blair replied:

> "As I said yesterday, the difficulties of a land force invasion of Kosovo against an undegraded Serb military machine are formidable, as they have been throughout. I have also said in the House before, and I repeat now, that Milosevic does not have a veto on NATO action. All options are always kept under review, and that is sensible for us to do. The right hon. Gentleman began his question by saying that, now we have embarked on the action, it has to succeed, and I agree that it has to succeed."[29]

For the first time, he told MPs publicly that ground troops were an option. Hours later, Blair flew to Washington for NATO's 50th anniversary celebrations. According to Kampfner, he asked his principal private secretary to arrange as many meetings with the US President and other senior members of his administration as possible to win the administration over for his plans, being well aware that US approval was essential for a NATO consensus on the use of ground troops. Yet his efforts were futile. After all, the US would have to share most of the

---

[25] House of Commons 1999: Debates, *Hansard* , 20/04/99, Columns 679 – 680,

[26] Ibid, Column 680

[27] House of Commons 1999: Debates, *Hansard* , 20/04/99, Column 681

[28] House of Commons 1999: *Hansard*, 21/04/99, Columns 899 - 900

[29] Ibid; BBC News 1999: "Ground Troops an Option – Blair", *BBC Online Network*, 21/04/99, http://news.bbc.co.uk/2/hi/uk_news/politics/324877.stm

burden of a ground invasion. According to one American official, Blair's efforts stretched his relation with Clinton to the point of becoming fraught as these efforts were perceived as an attempt "to lecture Bill", which was "counter-productive".[30] Whatever the details of his efforts to persuade Clinton were, he did consider the option of ground troops and brought it up in the House of Commons once a search for options alternative to aerial bombing ensued. This advocacy for the option to use ground forces indicates a strategic culture providing for preferences to use force decisively despite high risks.

The following day, on 24 April, Blair held a seminal speech before the Chicago Economic Club that summed up his approach to foreign, security and defence policy. It reaffirms the two driving forces behind his policy, the combination of humanitarianism and expediency. "We are witnessing the beginnings of a new doctrine of international community", he asserted. "We have learned twice before in this century that appeasement does not work. If we let an evil dictator range unchallenged, we will have to spill infinitely more blood and treasure to stop him later." And "We are all internationalists now, whether we like it or not". This internationalism or the new doctrine of international community stands for an alert concern for the welfare and security of others that does not stem purely from altruism, but also from a conviction that one's own welfare and security depends on it. This conviction is not entirely new, neither to British foreign policy nor to that of other European or 'Western' countries. The rigorous and proactive nature with which New Labour pursued its convictions constitutes the idiosyncrasy.

This is not to say that strategic culture causes British foreign policy decision-makers to act the way in which the Blair government acted towards the Kosovo tragedy 1998/99. Foreign, defence and security policy behaviour fluctuates with different administrations. The contrast between John Major's realist and Tony Blair's idealist external policy highlights this. However, these fluctuations are embedded in a social and cultural context, operate within certain margins and require elites and a public that goes along with their decisions. Major may have been rather reserved in his commitment of forces to Bosnia but Britain still committed relatively many. Blair may have stretched the limits of British strategic culture but it still provided the necessary conditions for his behaviour. In New Labour's foreign policy one can discern a strong belief in the efficacy of military force to achieve a broad range of objectives and a preference for the decisive use of force indicating a risk tolerance regarding casualties. In addition to this, the degree of autonomy with which the Blair government could operate and the quasi consensual nature with which the use of force was debated in the context of the Kosovo tragedy all very strongly suggest that British strategic culture provided the necessary condition for Tony Blair's government to put his idealism into practice. On 21 April 1997 during an election campaign speech in Manchester he reportedly stated:

> "The Britain in my vision is not Britain turning its back on the world – narrow, shy, uncertain. It is a Britain confident of its place in the world, sure of itself, able to negotiate with the world and provide leadership to the world. … Century upon century it has been the destiny of Britain to lead other nations. That should not be a destiny that is part of our history. It should be part of our future. We are a leader of nations or nothing."[31]

And in a guest essay published in *Newsweek* magazine on 14 June 1999 he wrote that "Milosevic has often in the past failed to deliver on the deals he signed. We need to hold Milosevic to this one and get the refugees back. We can then embark on a new moral crusade to rebuild the Balkans without him."[32] It is hard to imagine German foreign, defence and security policy decision-makers using such terminology.

---

[30] Kampfner 2003, p. 50

[31] Quoted in Kampfner 2003, p. 3; see also Keen, David 2007: "Labour's love's lost", *Le Monde Diplomatique* (May), available online at http://mondediplo.com/2007/05/18labour

[32] Blair, Tony 1999: "A New Moral Crusade", *Newsweek*, 14/06/1999, p. 35; see also Kampfner 2003, p. 60

5.1.2 The German decision to participate in OAF:

The German government's decision to participate in Operation Allied Force with 14 Tornado jets ultimately flying around 500 sorties is often regarded as an indication of Germany breaking with its self-imposed *Sonderrolle*, its rigorous rejection to participate in any combat operations. Especially the USA and Germany's Western partners saw it as a sign of growing maturity and the Federal Republic's transition to normality in its foreign, defence and security policy.[33] At first glance such an appraisal seems pertinent. Despite the absence of a UN Security Council mandate, Germany decided for the first time since the Second World War to participate in a combat operation. The campaign was conducted while a red-green coalition government was in power, with the Greens, a party with deeply pacifist roots, providing the foreign minister. On 16 October 1998, after a debate largely devoid of controversy, the Bundestag decided to participate in a limited air campaign planned by NATO and implemented in phases to prevent a humanitarian catastrophe in the Kosovo conflict by 500 votes for, 62 against and 18 abstentions.[34] This was a landmark decision indicative of a change in German thinking on the use of military force, its strategic culture. Nevertheless, at second glance, a distinct strategic culture that provided necessary condition for distinctive preferences and restraints regarding the use of force is still discernible.

Germany developed its decision to use force against Serbia later than its allies. Germany did not play an initiating, proactive but a rather passive, reactive role when it came to developing a consensus within NATO on the use of force against Serbia over the summer of 1998. While the UK government issued warnings to Milosevic and asked the Ministry of Defence to investigate plans for a ground invasion, the German government did not advocate the use of force against Serbia. The Kohl government dealt with the Kosovo conflict largely in the context of multilateral forums such as the Contact Group, the EU's Common Foreign and Security Policy (CFSP) and NATO.[35] As Germany received heavy criticism for its early recognition of Croatia in 1991 it consciously avoided any *Alleingang*. As Krause put it: „Die Hauptmaxime war, im europäischen und transatlantischen ‚Geleitzug' zu operieren und wenig Einzelaktionen und Initiativen zu wagen".[36] Its aims were to resolve the crisis through diplomatic means, while at the same time the government assured that it would not remain impassive in the face of a humanitarian catastrophe. At the same time it sought not to isolate and come in conflict with Russia as well as to reduce the continuous flow of Albanian refugees into Germany and the EU.[37] When hostilities increased in Kosovo in February and March 1998 it became increasingly difficult to reconcile these aims with each other. When calls from the United Kingdom and the US for the use of force became louder, the German Foreign Minister Klaus Kinkel adopted a mediating position between them and Russia. Throughout the debate on the use of force within NATO and the Contact Group the Kohl government and Kinkel in particular insisted on the need for a UN resolution authorisation NATO action although it became clear that Russia would not approve any such resolution.[38] This insistence only began crumbling in mid-August 1998 when the German Defence Minister Volker Rühe suggested in a newspaper interview that if necessary, a military intervention should occur without Security Council approval.[39] When the Security Council passed resolution 1199 on 23 September the UK and the US saw this resolution as authorising NATO to implement its demands in the case of Serb non-compliance. When NATO issued its Activation Warning the day after the North

[33] Krause, Joachim 2000: "Deutschland und die Kosovo-Krise", in: Reuter, Jens/Clewing, Conrad (ed.) 2000: "Der Kosovo Konflikt. Ursachen, Verlauf, Perspektiven", Wieser Verlag, Klagenfurt, p. 395.
[34] Deutscher Bundestag 1998: Plenary Protocol 13/248, 16/10/98, p. 23161, dip.bundestag.de/btp/13/13248.pdf
[35] Krause 2000, p. 400.
[36] Ibid, p. 396.
[37] Krause 2000, p. 400.
[38] Krause 2000, pp. 405 – 406.
[39] Ibid.

Atlantic Council asked its member states to state their troop commitments. On 30 September the Kohl government's last cabinet meeting decided to commit 14 Tornado jets although there were still doubts within the government about the legality of this action.[40] This cautious, reactive manner in which Germany decided to join OAF indicates several effects of its distinct strategic culture. It highlights that although Germany was determined to act against a humanitarian crisis there were great reservations about the use of force without UN authorisation. This option did not feature high on preference rankings. The use of ground troops was not considered at all, which indicates preferences for restraint in the use of force. The emphasis on international law and the UN as well as the legalistic character of German argumentation indicates a strong preference for the rule of law in international relations. Lastly, the reactive 'convoy' position Germany adopted in international debates on the use of force in Kosovo indicates a strong normative attachment to multilateralism. As Hyde-Price put it: "Particularly for a country like Germany, whose identity and national role conceptions are intimately bound up with multilateralism, foreign policy is constrained by international commitments to allies and partners."[41] These preferences are in line with Germany's identity as a civilian power. They differ sharply from the UK's early and proactive advocacy of the intensive use of force.

The subsequent debate in the *Bundestag* recaptured Germany's discernible norms, preferences and identities. Though there was widespread agreement that military force was necessary, with notable exceptions from the PDS fraction and some members of the Green Party and the Social Democrat Party, it was repeatedly emphasised that this decision was not an easy one but that all other options were exhausted and that the urgency of the situation in Kosovo demands this exceptional decision, which must not set a precedent. Kinkel for instance stated that "The bargaining potential is exhausted, the use of force is *ultima ratio.*"
Furthermore,

> "With its decision NATO did not create a new legal instrument, which could justify a general power of NATO for interventions, neither did it want to. NATO's decision must not set a precedent. We must not be delinquent regarding the Security Council's monopoly on the legitimate use of force."[42]

Fischer later reiterated Kinkel's remarks that this was an emergency situation, an exception rather than a precedent. Indeed, the word precedent was mentioned altogether thirty times during the debate. Kinkel also mentioned his uneasiness with the lack of a clear legal basis for NATO's action, as many others did:

> "I did not make it easy for myself either, if I may add, regarding the legal basis of NATO's orders; the colleagues in the House know my opinion. But I believe after careful study that the path which has now been taken by the 16 NATO partners is legally justifiable."[43]

Furthermore, in arguments justifying the use of force humanitarianism played as much a role as alliance solidarity. It was frequently argued that Germany must prove itself as a reliable ally. Lastly, deputies of all parliamentary parties highlighted that their consent concerned the limited use of air forces and not other eventualities such as ground operations.[44]

---

[40] Ibid, p. 407.
[41] Hyde-Price 2001, p. 21.
[42] „Die Verhandlungsmöglichkeiten sind erschöpft, der Einsatz von Gewalt ist Ultima ratio." Furthermore, „Mit ihrem Beschluß hat die NATO kein neues Rechtsinstrument geschaffen und auch nicht schaffen wollen, das eine Generalvollmacht der NATO für Interventionen begründen könnte. Der Beschluss der NATO darf nicht zum Präzedenzfall werden. Wir dürfen nicht auf eine schiefe Bahn kommen, was das Gewaltmonopol des Sicherheitsrates anbelangt." Deutscher Bundestag 1998: Plenary Protocol 13/248, 16/10/98, p. 23141
[43] Translation by the author, original in German: „Ich habe es auch mir selber nicht einfach gemacht - wenn ich das hinzufügen darf -, was die rechtliche Absicherung dessen betrifft, was von der NATO angeordnet worden ist; die Kolleginnen und Kollegen hier im Haus kennen meine Auffassung ja. Ich glaube aber nach eingehender Prüfung, daß der Weg, der von den 16 NATO-Partnern jetzt begangen worden ist, rechtlich vertretbar ist." Ibid.
[44] Krause 2000, p. 14.

Both the quantity and the quality of the German debate indicate that Germany's strategic culture helped to shape a preference for the restrained use of force for humanitarian purposes in accordance with international law as well as extensive domestic authorisation requirements and in close cooperation with international organisations, allies and partners after other options can be ruled out with certainty. Beliefs in the efficacy of military force to resolve the Kosovo tragedy were not as strong as in the UK. The German decision process and debate on the use of force against Serbia indicate that its strategic culture provided the necessary conditions for the restraint with which it participated in OAF.

5.1.2.1 Revising OAF in Germany:

In contrast to the UK, the German debate on the use of force in Kosovo was extensive, confronted Germany with many questions devoid of quick and simple answers and caused Germany to play a rather passive role in multilateral decision processes. This greater reluctance and unease with which Germany eventually decided to use force is also visible in the deep divisions that existed over Kosovo. The struggle between arguments for and against was not necessarily played out in parliament but rather within political parties, between politicians and the public and partly even between individuals themselves. Eventually, as the writer Peter Schneider has argued, those supporting and those opposing intervention went through the same inner struggle ("*Seelenstreit*").[45] These deep divisions and the complexity of the German debate, which contrast to the British debate, indicate a lower proclivity to justify the use of force in Germany. These deep divisions came to the fore particularly drastically when OAF did not deliver the desired results as quickly and therefore came under review. They highlight how German strategic culture provided the necessary conditions for Germany's continuing emphasis on diplomacy and its rejection of more combative options.

Shortly after the Kosovo debate in the *Bundestag* the red-green government under Chancellor Gerhard Schröder and Foreign Minister Joschka Fischer was sworn in on 27 October 1998. For this government the Kosovo War posed a huge dilemma. On the one hand they shared strong humanitarian concerns and sentiments of a responsibility to act with Germany's allies and partners, as they stated in the debate in the *Bundestag*, on the other hand they were not as convinced about the efficacy of military force to pursue these humanitarian interests and though they deemed the use of force for humanitarian purposes justified and necessary non-military means to resolve the crisis in Kosovo featured very highly on preference rankings. As *Die Zeit* noted, "traumas, scepticism and the political lessons of the last decades are certainly present in the collective consciousness".[46]

One indication that German strategic culture generated collective expectations and preference rankings that were not as strongly in favour of the use of force as in the UK is the time and effort spent by the Schröder government on justifying the use of force against Serbia once the air campaign was under way. Both the SPD and the Greens held special party conferences to discuss the government's position on the Kosovo War on 12 April and 13 May 1999 respectively. Especially within the Greens calls for an immediate end to the bombing campaign grew louder as it progressed. Fischer faced particularly strong demands to justify his position as it constituted a break with his party's and his own pacifist roots. In 1994 he wrote:

> "... due to the special German history this country is well-advised not to pursue a return to a military-based foreign policy. Germany was fully alliance-capable without power politics and 'out-of-area'-missions for centuries and will continue to do so under a majority, which rejects Germany's return to military-based power politics for good reasons. One would knowingly give up one of the greatest achievements of the

---

[45] Schneider, Peter 1999: "Eiserne Mienen", *Frankfurter Allgemeine Zeitung*, 23/04/99, p. 43; quoted in Hyde-Price 2001, p. 31.

[46] *Die Zeit*, 31/04/99, p. 6; quoted in Hyde-Price 2001, p. 31.

post-World War II-era, which is the break with the Prussian-German tradition of the authoritarian state and the concentration of the democratic Germany on civilian politics."[47]

Although Fischer along with the overwhelming majority of German decision-makers abandoned its strict pacifism since Bosnia, turning the maxim *nie wieder Krieg* (never again war) into *nie wieder Auschwitz* (never again Auschwitz) this culturally-rooted scepticism about the use of force prevailed amongst many Green Party members. At the Green Party's special party conference in Bielefeld on 13 May 1999 the moderate strand of its party base prevailed with its demand for a temporary halt of the bombing campaign over more radical factions demanding an immediate end to air strikes the conference took a riotous course. According to his autobiography, in which he called the Kosovo War a 'red-green nightmare' Fischer was determined to resign, which would mean that a new government would have to be formed if his party disapproved of his policy over Kosovo.[48] This friction between Fischer and parts of his party base highlights the presence of normative concerns about military force that deeply divided the German public and rendered the debate over air strikes a highly complex one.
Another indication of different collective expectations and preference rankings can be found in Germany's herein before-mentioned resolute rejection of ground troops and its ongoing emphasis on diplomacy. When public support for military means crumbled as the bombing campaign lasted longer than anticipated Germany pursued a twin-track approach of a continuing commitment to OAF combined with intensive diplomatic efforts while categorically rejecting the option of a ground invasion. On 15 April, after Schroeder gave a government declaration on the current situation in Kosovo, a debate ensued in which members of government as well as opposition parties rejected the use of ground troops because this would be counterproductive to finding a political solution and bear incalculable risks of heavy casualties and an escalation of the conflict, including a possible confrontation with Russia. The Bavarian Premier Edmund Stoiber of the CDU/CSU fraction stated that

> "A large, a vast majority of the German population is afraid of and worried about possible deployments of … combat troops on the ground. I enunciate this before this Honourable House so that the people know the position. Such a deployment would inevitably obstruct those political options, which we need to solve the problems. CDU and CSU as well as the Federal Government have therefore clearly argued against the deployment of NATO combat troops on the ground in this conflict. We must not utilise means, which obstruct, if not render impossible, political solutions and whose consequences we cannot control. We must make this position clear, not only here but also within the alliance."[49]

Gernot Erler from the Social Democrats even said that it is Germany's responsibility to prevent the deployment of ground troops to Serbia:

---

[47] Translation by the author, original in German: „… aus der besonderen deutschen Geschichte heraus ist dieses Land nun einmal gut beraten, keine Rückkehr zu einer militärisch gestützten Außenpolitik zu betreiben. Deutschland war auch ohne Weltpolitik und „out-of-area"-Einsätze über Jahrzente hinweg voll bündnisfähig und ein allseits geachtetes Mitglied der westlichen Staatengemeinschaft und wird dies auch unter einer Mehrheit bleiben, die Deutschlands Rückweg in eine militärisch gestützte Weltpolitik aus guten Gründen ablehnt. (…) Sehenden Auges würde man eine der größten Errungenschaften der Nachkriegszeit aufgeben, nämlich den Bruch mit der preußisch-deutschen Machtstaatstradition und die Konzentration des demokratischen Deutschlands auf die zivile Politik". Fischer 1994, p. 229

[48] Fischer, Joschka 2007: „Die rot-grünen Jahre", Kiepenheuer & Witsch, Cologne, p. 221.

[49] Translation by the author, original in German: „eine große, eine überwältigende Mehrheit der deutschen Bevölkerung [hat] Sorge und Angst vor möglichen Einsätzen von … Bodenkampftruppen. Dies spreche ich in diesem Hohen Haus … sehr deutlich aus, damit die Menschen die Positionen kennen. Ein solcher Einsatz würde zwangsläufig gerade die politischen Optionen verbauen, die wir zur Lösung der Probleme benötigen. CDU und CSU haben sich deshalb ebenso wie die Bundesregierung klar gegen den Einsatz von Bodenkampftruppen der NATO in diesem Konflikt ausgesprochen. Wir dürfen keine Mittel einsetzen, die politische Lösungen erschweren oder sogar unmöglich machen und die wir in den Konsequenzen nicht beherrschen können. Diesen Standpunkt müssen wir nicht nur hier, sondern auch innerhalb des Bündnisses immer wieder deutlich machen." Deutscher Bundestag 1999: Plenary Protocol 14/32, 14/04/99, pp. 2642 – 2645, http://dip.bundestag.de/btp/14/14032.pdf

"Due to our historical responsibility alone we must do everything so that there will never be another deployment of ground troops to Yugoslavia."[50]

The *New York Times* reported on 20 May 1999 that at a news conference in Brussels "Mr. Schroeder lambasted the debate in Britain over sending ground troops into Kosovo".[51] It is remarkable how the levels of support for the option to use ground troops differed fundamentally between the British and the German parliament, with some advocacy for this option in the House of Commons and outright rejection in the *Bundestag*.

Inherent in Germany's diplomatic efforts was the use of multilateral bodies to reach a solution. While holding the EU presidency Germany brought forward the idea of a stability pact for South-East Europe to prevent reoccurrences of the Kosovo tragedy at a special Kosovo summit in April in Cologne. Within the 'Quint', a group consisting of all Contact Group members except for Russia, and the G8 Germany was active in forging and rallying support for a set of conditions for the cessation of air strikes. In its diplomatic efforts Germany tried to include the UN, China and especially Russia to render its Kosovo policy more legal and legitimate.[52] This can be seen on its invitation of then-UN General Secretary Kofi Annan to the EU special summit in Cologne on 14 April followed by a three-day visit to Germany and the "steady stream of German diplomats and political leaders travelling to Moscow to encourage the Russian government to play a positive role in the conflict" as well as Germany's efforts to encourage Washington to intensify its dialogue with Moscow.[53] Fischer's peace plan proposed in early April encapsulates Germany's diplomatic endeavours.[54] It envisaged a 24 hour break in NATO bombing in return for a Serb withdrawal from Kosovo followed by international efforts for a political settlement that incorporated China and Russia, thereby isolating Serbia, and a range of socio-economic measures to stabilise the region as a whole. It was not accepted by Germany's partners.[55]

The increasing friction between political elites and the public during OAF coupled with strong efforts of the Schröder government to justify aerial bombardments and to find a diplomatic solution to the conflict signify that its decision to participate in OAF came at some political costs. Norms and public expectations in Germany generated strong preferences for diplomatic options to pursue its interests to end the Kosovo crisis. This contrasts sharply with the Blair government's preference for the option to use more intensive military means to pursue the same interest. In both cases the effects of distinct strategic cultures providing necessary conditions for distinct behaviour towards Kosovo in 1998 and 1999 are discernible.

---

[50] Translation by the author, original in German: „Schon aus unserer historischen Verantwortung heraus müssen wir alles tun, damit es nie mehr zum Einsatz von Bodentruppen in Jugoslawien kommt." Ibid, p. 2653

[51] Cohen 1999.

[52] Longhurst 2004, p. 72.

[53] Hyde-Price 2001, p. 28.

[54] Longhurst 2004, p. 72.

[55] Ibid, pp. 72 – 73.

5.1.3 Summarising and synthesising the findings

Chapter 3 showed that elites and the public in both the UK and Germany consider the use of force for humanitarian purposes justified. It also showed that German and British elites differ in beliefs about the efficacy of military means relative to non-military means, the intensity with which force should be used, the necessity of international and domestic authorisation requirements to the use of force and on normative attachments to multilateralism. In the decision process and debates in the run up to OAF as well as in debates and decision processes during OAF the UK's and Germany's respective preferences differed in correlation with differences in the four components of their respective strategic culture. In both countries there was a consensus amongst elites that military force for humanitarian purposes was necessary and justified in this case. The UK justified the use of force on humanitarian grounds and security interests by referring to the failure of appeasement. In Germany humanitarian arguments as well as arguments about international commitments and responsibilities towards its allies played a large role. One could discern a stronger preference for the use of force in the UK, which advocated and prepared for its employment at an early stage. The quantitative scope of debates in the UK was relatively small and decision-makers could act with relative autonomy. The lack of a clear UN mandate appeared significantly more problematic in Germany than in the UK and the scope of debates was larger in Germany. One could discern a preference for non military means and, second to that, a preference for the restrained use of force involving low risks of casualties. The final decisions reflected these preferences, with the UK committing significantly more troops and machinery. When aerial bombardments did not prove as effective as anticipated the alternative options considered in Germany and the UK differed fundamentally, with the UK favouring and advocating more drastic military measures and Germany advocating and pursuing diplomatic means. This all indicates that different strategic cultures helped to shape different, ranked sets of options for the pursuit of the aim to put an end to the Kosovo tragedy.

5.2 Comparing British and German military interventions in Africa

This chapter will compare and contrast two recent but separate instances of military interventions. Both the British military intervention in Sierra Leone and the German military intervention in the Democratic Republic of Congo are instances of recent military interventions in Africa. These instances are characteristic of each country's strategic cultures and their effect on behaviour.

5.2.1 The British military intervention in Sierra Leone

As it has been argued before, a strategic culture allowing a state a sufficient proclivity to use force is a necessary condition for humanitarian interventions. This section will argue that British strategic culture provided this condition to the British military intervention in Sierra Leone in 2000. One problem with this endeavour is that the decision process to deploy British troops "in the largest unilateral overseas military operation since the Falklands war" is hard to trace since it was a very quick decision. Another problem is that debates on this intervention took place only after troops were deployed. The first time that Foreign Secretary Robin Cook informed the House of Commons that the UK is to intervene in Sierra Leone was on 8 May 2000, one day after troop deployment. Yet this in itself is already strongly indicative.

As chapter 3 and the previous section on events surrounding the Kosovo crisis 1998/99 showed, British strategic culture contains a higher proclivity to the use of force in all four norm dimensions in comparison to German strategic culture. This leads to collective expectations allowing for shorter and more proactive decision processes, less intense debates and preferences for options involving the intensive use of military force to pursue security and defence policy goals, which ultimately result in decisions to do so. When this decision comes under review, British strategic culture allows for options involving military operations of higher intensity to be considered. In the run up to and during the British military intervention in Sierra Leone 2000 these processes can be observed.

What a strategic culture based explanation cannot account for is why a specific intervention took place at a specific time. Various contextual factors such events abroad, the administration in power, the degree of media attention shed on a specific event etc. might provide sufficient conditions. This book cannot account for why the UK intervened in Sierra Leone in 2000 but not in other African civil wars and genocides at other places and times. It can account for why the UK used force intensively in Sierra Leone. Yet before the decision process and debates in the run up to the intervention can be traced, a short review of the factors that explain why this relatively little-known intervention came into question in the first place may be permitted.

On 12 May 1997 Robin Cook gave a seminal speech intended to be a mission statement for the newly elected Labour government's foreign policy. It stated that he sought to introduce "an ethical content to foreign policy and recognize that national interest cannot be defined only by narrow *realpolitik*".[56] This maxim, which was already detectable in the Kosovo War, became a fundamental driving force in British foreign policy towards Sierra Leone. On 25 May the democratically elected President of Sierra Leone, Ahmed Tejan Kabbah, was overthrown by junior army officers, which then formed an Armed Forces Revolutionary Council (AFRC) and invited the Revolutionary United Front (RUF) to join their administration, making their leader Foday Sankoh its vice-chairman. The RUF was a notorious rebel group known for having indulged in most vicious acts of brutality against civilians. The mayhem and chaos ensuing the RUF's march on Freetown in May 1997 were relayed live on TV in London and

[56] quoted from Kargbo, Michael 2006: "British Foreign Policy in Sierra Leone", Peter Lang, Bern, p. 262.

other Western capitals.[57] This event thus provided an early test to New Labour's pledge to an internationalist foreign policy, which it could therefore not easily ignore. The Blair government sought to help Kabbah return from exile in Guinea. Yet at this point it intervened only indirectly. The Economic Community of West African States (ECOWAS) formed a monitoring group (ECOMOG) mostly consistent of Nigerian army personnel that sought to restore Kabbah to office by force. The UK supported this force with US$ 7million for logistical support, maps and intelligence sharing but refused more direct support because of its dismay of Nigeria's then-president Sani Abacha's poor human rights record.[58] In addition, the British Foreign and Commonwealth Office (FCO) or at least its High Commissioner to Sierra Leone, Peter Penfold, colluded with the mercenary firm Sandline International, to supply Kabbah with arms. By February 1998 ECOMOG forces then dispelled the RUF from Freetown and Kabbah returned to power. Yet UN Resolution 1132 of 8 October 1997, which The UK drafted and voted for, banned the supply of arms to Sierra Leone. When the FCO's collusion with Sandline International leaked to the press it became known as the "Arms-to-Africa" affair.[59] Defending himself Blair told the press on 11 May:

> "Let's not forget that both the UN and the UK were trying to help the democratically elected regime to restore its position from an illegal military coup. It was a democratically elected regime that people were trying to help. They were quite right in trying to do it. Nobody should ever act in breach of a UN arms embargo, but Mr Penfold did a superb job last year in dealing with the consequences of the May coup. That is the background, and people can see that a lot of the hoo-ha is overblown.[60]

Yet Kabbah's return was short-lived. In January 1999 the RUF ravaged over Freetown again with its notorious brutality. In July 1999 Kabbah, under the auspices of a British-led International Contact Group, signed a questionable peace agreement, which granted the RUF a general amnesty and installed their leader, Sankoh, as vice-president in charge of strategic minerals such as diamonds. A UN peacekeeping mission, UNAMSIL, was to replace Nigerian ECOMOG troops and to oversee this agreement. This so-called Lomé Agreement soon unravelled and the UN mission could not reduce the appalling levels of violence in Sierra Leone for very long. In May 2000 alarming reports reached the FCO that up to 500 UN soldiers were taken hostage and the RUF was about to take Freetown again.[61]

It is against this background of previous engagement that the British decision to deploy troops in May 2000 has to be seen. Britain intervened in the civil war in Sierra Leone before, although in a privatised form, and committed itself to support Kabbah. For Blair these ends justified the means to breach an arms embargo. This pragmatic, proactive and autonomous stile of security and defence policy in itself already hints at certain traits of British strategic culture. Blair's depiction of the Arms-to-Africa scandal as an 'overblown hoo-ha' suggests that collective expectations stemming from British strategic culture were not too incompatible with his policy towards Sierra Leone until then.

Little is known about the decision process immediate to the deployment of troops in May 2000. It appears to have been a sudden, spontaneous decision whose main catalyst was a "panic-stricken report" filed by the UN based on information provided by UNAMSIL and backed up by intelligence gathered from the new British High Commissioner David Jones and a British 15 man "Technical Assistance Team" attached to UNAMSIL that the RUF and other rebels were once again intent to capture Freetown. According to the *Guardian* this intelligence was in part contradictory and the decision to intervene thus taken "against a confused,

[57] Ibid, p. 269.

[58] Williams, Paul 2001: "Fighting for Freetown", *Contemporary Security Policy*, 22:3, p. 147

[59] Kargbo 2006, pp. 262 – 279; Williams 2001, pp. 145 – 147; Kampfner 2003, pp. 65 – 69.

[60] Abrams, Fran 1998: "Blair: 'We did nothing wrong", *The Independent*, 12/05/98; also quoted in Kargbo 2006, p. 279; Williams 2005, p. 82 and Kampfner 2003, p. 68.

[61] Kargbo 2006, pp. 285 - 297; Williams 2001, pp. 147 - 153; Williams 2005, pp. 82 - 83; Kampfner 2003, pp. 68 - 70.

chaotic and fast-moving background."[62] Kargbo and Williams reject allegations of flawed evidence and state that there was a significant threat to citizens in Freetown, 500 British citizens and up to 500 UNAMSIL forces captured by rebels.[63] In any case, the UK decided to intervene in Sierra Leone hastily. According to the *Guardian* first reports of a deteriorating situation reached the FCO on 1 May.[64] The *Washington Post* reported on 6 and 7 May 2000 8that rebels killed and captured UNAMSIL forces and were approaching Freetown in stolen UN vehicles.[65] In his statement on Sierra Leone on Monday, 8 May Cook revealed to MPs that a spearhead battalion of 700 men alongside the aircraft carrier HMS Illustrious and the amphibious assault ship HMS Ocean, support vessels and a number of helicopters were deployed to Sierra Leone over the weekend and the High Commission has activated its evacuation plan this afternoon.[66]

This short decision process accompanied by virtually no prior parliamentary debate is exemplary. It does not only highlight the peculiarity of the Royal Prerogative but also the relative ease with which the UK decides to employ its military force. This indicates that British strategic culture entails a relatively high proclivity to the use of force. Furthermore, the autonomous character of the decision process to intervene reveals once again a proactive stile of security and defence policy, which indicates a strategic culture that allows for *Alleingänge*. After all, despite Security Council condemnation of RUF incursions and Annan's repeated warnings in the week from 1 to 7 May 2000 that "the deteriorating situation in Sierra Leone - combined with the unwillingness of the United States and European powers to intervene - threatens to undercut international support for peacekeeping throughout Africa"[67] the UK was the only country to intervene alongside the beleaguered UN forces. Before the House of Commons on 8 May Cook argued the deployments took place

> "... to safeguard the security of British nationals. Our forces will ensure the security of the international Sierra Leone airport. Not only is that of immediate utility for the evacuation, but it is valuable in allowing the UN forces to continue to build up."[68]

He thus based his arguments on self-interested as well as humanitarian motives, which were the evacuation of British citizens and those to whom Britain had consular responsibility as well as support to UN troops. Cook concluded that "We must not allow a few thousand rebels to prevent the end to violence, and the peace in which to get on with their lives for which 3 million people in Sierra Leone desperately hunger."[69] The House generally welcomed the launch of Operation Palliser but the Conservative opposition demanded clarity on the mandate as it suspected that the purpose of the mission went beyond evacuation. Thus the foreign affairs spokesman Francis Maude stated that he strongly supports the decision but:

> "Given the evidence that Britain's armed forces are already stretched dangerously thin, will the Foreign Secretary make it categorically clear that the British contingent in Sierra Leone has one mandate, and one mandate only: to get the British nationals out? Will he assure the House that the sending of, effectively, three battalion strengths of the Parachute Regiment and Marines, as well as five ships - plus, we are now

[62] MacAskill, Ewan/Norton-Taylor, Richard 2000: "Flawed evidence led to 'mission creep'", *The Guardian*, 16/05/2000, http://www.guardian.co.uk/Archive/Article/0,4273,4018568,00.html; Kargbo 2006 pp. 297 – 298; Williams 2005, p. 83.

[63] Kargbo 2006 pp. 297 – 298; Williams 2001, pp. 153 – 154; Williams 2005, p. 83.

[64] MacAskill/Norton-Taylor 2000

[65] Lynch, Colum 2000a: "UN Force Crumbles In Sierra Leone, Peacekeepers Begin Surrender to Rebels", *Washington Post*, 06/05/2000, p. 1; Lynch, Colum 2000b: "Rebels Advance Toward Freetown, Reports Differ on UN Clashes With Sierra Leone Insurgents", *Washington Post*, 07/05/2000, p. 1.

[66] House of Commons 2000a: Debates, *Hansard*, Column 518, 08/05/2000, http://www.publications.parliament.uk/pa/cm199900/cmhansrd/vo000508/debtext/00508-11.htm,

[67] Lynch 2000a.

[68] House of Commons 2000a, Column 519.

[69] Ibid.

told, an aircraft carrier - is for that purpose only, and not part of a wider military commitment to shore up a United Nations operation that appears to be close to collapse?"[70]

Cook did not deliver the demanded assurance in his reply:

> I entirely echo what the right hon. Gentleman said about the brutal, nasty nature of the RUF and the need to contain it, and that is why I invite him to reflect again on the language that he used about the UN operation. The message from the House should not be that we are about to accept the collapse of the UN operation or that, reading between the lines, we might be secretly gratified to see its collapse. We all want to work to make a success of that operation, and Britain will take every step that we can to do so.[71]

He thus made it clear that the mission's objectives go beyond securing the evacuation of British nationals. This preference for and firm belief in the efficacy of the decisive use of military force to achieve Britain's security and defence policy goal of containing the RUF despite the high risks involved as well as the autonomy with which the government could act and the relatively unilateral nature of this decision all show that strategic culture provided necessary conditions for this decision to come about.

Another indication that norms generate collective expectations that allow for decision-makers to hold preferences for such actions can be found in how the parliament debated the gradual extension of its mandate as the operation proceeded. Soon after deployment the number of British troops in Sierra Leone reached a total of 1,300. After securing the airport and the evacuation of British and other citizens British troops assisted the deployment of further UNAMSIL personnel until the mission reached its originally authorised strength of 11,000 and secured the area around Freetown. [72] This involved some engagements with rebels and rebel casualties.[73] British Special Forces also helped to capture the RUF's leader Foday Sankoh in Freetown on 17 May.[74] It was only on 7 June that Cook revealed the mission's operations in their entirety to the House of Commons.[75] Rather than being accused of "mission-creep", an American term used to describe the gradual expansion of a mission beyond its original mandate until it gets further and further drawn into a conflict[76], parliamentarians expressed their unequivocal consent of the course the mission has taken. Francis Maude thus said:

> "The House will want to join in congratulating our soldiers on their role. They have, as we have come to expect, discharged their duties with calm and distinction. As the right hon. Gentleman knows, we have been ready to support whatever tasks they might be asked to undertake."[77]

Although his critique would probably have turned out differently if Cook presented a different operational record the decision process to launch Operation Palliser and the debates subsequent to its launch highlight that British foreign, defence and security policy decision-makers can decide to use military force with relative ease. Although originally the mission's rationale was to evacuate British citizens the sheer scale of the deployment already indicated that it intended to do more. As *The Times* correctly asserted on 10 May:

---

[70] House of Commons 2000a, column 520.

[71] Ibid, column 521.

[72] Williams 2001, pp. 83 – 84.

[73] Ibid

[74] "Paras kill Sierra Leone rebels", *BBC News*, 17 May 2000, http://news.bbc.co.uk/2/hi/uk_news/752292.stm; "Rebel leader in secret custody", *BBC News*, 17 May 2000, http://news.bbc.co.uk/2/hi/africa/751912.stm

[75] House of Commons 2000b: Debates, *Hansard*, 07/06/2000, columns 161 – 163, http://www.publications.parliament.uk/pa/cm199900/cmhansrd/vo000606/debtext/00606-05.htm; see also Williams 2005, p. 155.

[76] On 8 May 2000 Francis Maude asked Robin Cook: "Is the Foreign Secretary familiar with the inelegant but illuminating American expression 'mission creep'? It describes a situation in which troops deployed for one purpose slowly, under pressure of events and with the best intentions, find themselves drawn into operations for which they are not prepared, trained or equipped.", Hansard 2000a, column 522

[77] Hansard 2000b, column 163.

> "Britain is not going to Sierra Leone merely to evacuate its nationals. It is going to show it cares about Africa, that wherever democracy is under threat and human lives are being lost, 'something must be done'. Why else has the carrier HMS Illustrious been diverted from duty? Why are 550 marines setting sail this week from Marseilles aboard the helicopter carrier HMS Ocean, as part of a full Amphibious Ready Group … Already four Chinooks are in the theatre, alongside eight C130 Hercules. … The fact must be that British soldiers are going to Sierra Leone to do more than evacuate civilians."[78]

But despite going well beyond its original evacuation purposes the mission could operate without parliamentary or public outcries. On the contrary, parliamentary approval of the mission increased as it expanded its mandate. This indicates that norms contained in British strategic culture generate some collective expectations that 'something must be done'. These expectations allow for decision-makers' preferences to use force intensively to pursue the security and defence policy goal of restoring peace and order in Sierra Leone.

It should also be noted that after the situation stabilised in mid-June 2000 and even after British troops were kidnapped in September, which was followed by a rescue operation that led to the death of approximately 25 enemy forces and one British soldier[79] the UK did not abandon its commitment to Sierra Leone. After the bulk of troops were withdrawn in June the UK left behind 200 troops to train an accountable and effective Sierra Leone army and increased its presence to 650 soldiers again in October to bolster UNAMSIL. If required, it pledged to deploy a further rapid reaction force of up to 5000 troops[80]. This suggests a firm belief in the utility of military force to pursue humanitarian goals and a high risk tolerance on behalf of British decision-makers.

[78] Jenkins, Simon 2000: "Stuck in the mire of the white man's burden", *The Times*, 10/05/2000; quoted from Kargbo 2006, p. 299.
[79] http://www.army.mod.uk/16_air_asslt_bde/deployments/operation_barras.htm
[80] Williams 2005, p. 83.

5.2.2 The German military intervention in the Democratic Republic of Congo

The German decision process to deploy approximately 750 soldiers to the Democratic Republic of Congo (DRC) as part of an EU force (EUFOR) contrasts sharply with the run up to the British decision process to deploy troops to Sierra Leone. It took place within a much longer time frame at the end of which Germany decided hesitantly and in response to requests by and pressure from multilateral institutions, allies and partners, to take the lead over this mission.[81] On 12 December 2003 EU member states adopted the European Security Strategy, a document which asserts that "Active policies are needed to counter the new dynamic threats. We need to develop a strategic culture that fosters early, rapid, and when necessary, robust intervention."[82] Taking the EU at its word, on 27 December 2005 the UN Under-Secretary General for Peacekeeping Operations Jean-Marie Guehénno asked the EU to provide troops to assist MONUC in providing security during, before and after the forthcoming parliamentary presidential elections in the DRC. After all, the EU was engaged in the DRC before. In June 2003 the French-led EU Operation Artemis reacted to Annan's calls for support of the UN Mission in Congo (MONUC) in the Bunia region.[83] And on 12 December 2005 the European Council reaffirmed its commitment to a peaceful, democratic and prosperous DRC.[84] Although Guehénno's request met widespread approval in the EU, member states could not decide on their troop contributions and on who will take the lead until mid-March.[85] Especially the German government and its Defence Minister Franz Josef Jung long hesitated to make a decision. In mid-February the EU's Military Committee (EUMC) drafted a piece of military advice by which, after its formal adoption, a commander and a headquarter would have to be announced for the mission, followed by a conference at which troop contributions were to be discussed. Germany asked for the adoption of this peace of advice to be postponed indefinitely because it wanted to wait for other member states to informally announce their participation first. But member states were reluctant to make statements on possible contributions prior to its formal adoption. This temporarily laid the decision process on ice.[86] At an informal meeting of EU defence ministers in Innsbruck, Austria on 7 and 8 March 2006 member states could still not agree on the size, scope and headquarter of the mission. France and the UK expressed their general support for this mission but conceded that their army headquarters in Northwood and Montelimar were not available due to other obligations. The UK referred to its engagement in Iraq and Afghanistan, arguing this would not leave it the necessary capacities. France referred to its prior lead role in Operation Artemis.[87] This mounted pressure on Germany to decide on the scope of its commitment to the planned mission. Germany did not declare a non-commitment on time and was one of the few member states with the capacity to take a lead role. A Franco-German summit on 14 March 2006 finally broke the impasse. The French President Jacques Chirac agreed to provide roughly as many troops as Germany. In this situa-

[81] See Schmidt, Peter 2006: „Freiwillige vor!", *Internationale Politik* (November), pp. 68 – 77; Bacia, Horst 2006: „Spring Du, ich schieße", *FAZ-NET*, 15/03/2006, article available online at www.faz.net

[82] European Union: "A Secure Europe in a Better World: European Security Strategy", Brussels, p. 11, document available online at http://ue.eu.int/uedocs/cmsUpload/78367.pdf.

[83] The UK supported this mission and encouraged France to Europeanise the operation rather than conduct it on a looser multilateral basis whereas German officials were more reluctant to consider the deployment of troops for fear that this would create a precedent for German interventions in Africa, thus raise negative connotations of a new *Afrikakorps*. See Miskimmon, Alister 2004: „Continuity in the Face of Upheaval – British strategic culture and the impact of the Blair government", *European Security* 13:3 (special issue), pp. 282 – 283.

[84] Council of the European Union 2005: Press Release 14960/05, 12/12/2005, pp. 13 – 15, document available online at http://www.fco.gov.uk/Files/kfile/eu2005_CC_GenAff_12dec,0.pdf; see also Schmidt 2006, p. 70.

[85] Schmidt 2006, p. 69.

[86] Bacia 2006.

[87] Schmidt 2006, pp. 69 – 70; Bacia 2006.

tion the German government could not elude a lead role.[88] On 27 April the Council of Ministers issued a Joint Action in which the German General Karlheinz Viereck was designated to be the mission's "Operation Commander" and Potsdam its headquarters.[89]
Yet the decision process was not over at this point. The government still had to decide on the specifics of the planned mission, which the parliament then had to approve of. On 17 May the Cabinet passed a motion to the *Bundestag* in which it spelled out these specifics. The German contribution to the total EUFOR size of approximately 2000 soldiers should consist of 500 militaries and 280 soldiers to provide logistical and medical support. These troops are to be stationed mainly in Gabon as 'on-call forces' to execute operations of limited character in order to extract individuals in danger.[90] They will remain for a total four months and only be deployed in and around Kinshasa.[91] On 1 June 2006 the *Bundestag* approved of this motion with 440 votes for it, 135 against and 6 abstentions, which cleared the road for deployment.

This long, extensive and intricate decision process is exemplary. The apparent reluctance with which the German government decided to take the lead of EUFOR DR Congo in response of a French initiative as well as the restrictions imposed upon its mandate show that German strategic culture contains a lower proclivity to the use of force in all four norm dimensions in comparison to British strategic culture. This leads to collective expectations requiring longer, more reactive decision processes, exhaustive debates and preferences for less risky options involving the restricted use of military force to pursue Germany's security and defence policy goals.
This is also discernible in the way in which the use of force in the DRC was debated in parliament. Unsurprisingly, as the subject of debate was an EU military operation, there were frequent references to the European Union. Yet these references stood in the context of arguments to justify the mission. These arguments were based on humanitarian grounds as well as references to commitments and responsibilities to Germany's allies and partners. Indeed, as Schmidt argues, "Critics had to be ready to be called opponents of the UN, of Franco-German relations and of the EU and thereby to place themselves outside the widely shared foreign policy consensus in German politics."[92] Fritz Kuhn from the Green Party faction for instance attacked the FDPs rejection of the government's motion on precisely these grounds:

> I ask the FDP, which – at least according to its self-image – is one of the most European parties, what it thinks of what the European Union itself decided in December 2005. (…) Now is the chance to say 'yes' to what we all believe to be programmatically right, to what we decided upon together in the European Union, thus at this first real litmus test and to help bringing a new perspective to the people in Congo. I cannot imagine that the members of the Bundestag will really say 'no' to this. **If the European Union wants to implement what it decided upon then this can only imply that we will endorse this mandate;** because we want to vitalise the partnership between the European Union and Africa."[93]

[88] Schmidt 2006, p. 70.
[89] Ibid, p. 71.
[90] The restriction of the mandate to only extract individuals in danger is however already contained in UN Security Council Resolution 8698, which authorises this mission. This document is available online at http://www.un.org/News/Press/docs/2006/sc8698.doc.htm; see also Schmidt 2006, p. 75.
[91] Deutscher Bundestag 2006a: Printed paper 16/1507, 17/05/2006, pp. 2 – 4, http://dip21.bundestag.de/dip21/btd/16/015/1601507.pdf; Schmidt 2006, p. 75.
[92] Translation by the author, original in German: „Kritiker mussten bereit sein, sich gleichzeitig als Opponenten der UN, der deutsch-französischen Beziehungen und der EU bezeichnen zu lassen und sich damit außerhalb des weithin geteilten außenpolitischen Konsenses in der deutschen Politik zu stellen." Schmidt 2006, p. 71.
[93] Emphasis added. Translation by the author, original in German: „Ich frage die FDP, die – jedenfalls nach ihrem Selbstverständnis – eine der europäischsten Parteien ist, was sie von dem hält, was die Europäische Union im Dezember 2005 selbst beschlossen hat. (…) Jetzt kommt es darauf an, zu dem, was wir alle für programmatisch richtig halten, zu dem, was wir gemeinsam in der Europäischen Union beschlossen haben, also bei diesem ersten wirklichen Lackmustest, Ja zu sagen und mitzuhelfen, den Menschen im Kongo eine neue Perspektive zu geben. Ich kann mir nicht vorstellen, dass Mitglieder des Deutschen Bundestages dazu tatsächlich Nein sagen. Wenn die Europäische Union das umsetzen will, was sie beschlossen hat, dann kann das nur bedeuten, dass wir diesem Mandat zustimmen werden; denn wir wollen die Partnerschaft zwischen der Europäischen Union und

These lines of argumentation reveal a recurring pattern present since the Gulf War in German debates on the use of force by which a strong normative attachment to multilateralism, to allies and partners, provides necessary conditions for instances of its restrained use of force. This normative attachment contained in German strategic culture generates preferences for multilateral actions and for compliance with responsibilities and commitments to partners and allies.

The debate also revealed strong normative reservations towards the use of force and its utility. The FDP and the Left fractions rejected the government's motion because they doubted the effectiveness of the planned deployments and argued non-military means such as assistance in the construction of a public infrastructure ("Aufbau staatlicher Strukturen") should come before military means are considered as a last resort.[94] Despite the constrains that the government imposed on the planned mission, probably in part to ensure parliamentary support, several concerns about the employment of military means such as a possible confrontation with child soldiers were raised. Petra Hinz from the SPD fraction thus argued:

> "Combat operations with child soldiers cannot be ruled out, the situation in Congo is anything but calm, people's reactions cannot be predicted on the ground. This means that in case of an emergency this mission will be a combat mission with an unknown opponent and ending. We should take seriously the concerns of those we deploy."[95]

In the last sentence she most likely referred to voices from within the *Bundeswehr* raising similar concerns about their expected deployment. The German debate on the *Bundeswehr*'s first deployment to Africa since its support for UNOSOM II in 1991 thus raised several issues and concerns that were not raised in the British debate on its deployment to Sierra Leone. In addition, these concerns were raised although the government's motion already counteracted them. Confrontations with child soldiers for example were made unlikely through the deployment's geographical and temporal restrictions, which avoided the more war-torn eastern provinces of the DRC. This highlights the peculiarities of German strategic thinking. Adrian Hyde-Price argued in the context of the German debate on Kosovo that it "demonstrated a maturity and seriousness found in very few other countries – and certainly contrasted favourably with the public debate in the USA or the UK."[96] The CDU parliamentarian Hans Reidel also asserted in the *Bundestag*'s debate on EUFOR DR Congo that there are peculiarities in German debates on the use of force but emphasised these differences in a more pejorative way:

> "The UN asked the EU to supply a contingent. The African Union supports this as well. In Congo even the politicians in charge agreed to support this process so that democratisation can advance. Still we – as the only ones in Europe – have this agonising debate. In no other country, neither in France nor anywhere else, is such a discussion being held."[97]

Afrika mit Leben erfüllen." Deutscher Bundestag 2006b: Plenary protocol 16/37, 01/06/2006, pp. 3244 – 3245, http://dip.bundestag.de/btp/16/16037.pdf

[94] Ibid, pp. 3238 – 3239, 3241 – 3243.

[95] Translation by the author, original in German: „Kampfhandlungen mit Kindersoldaten können nicht ausgeschlossen werden, die Lage im Kongo ist alles andere als ruhig, die Reaktionen der Bevölkerung können im Ernstfall nicht eingeschätzt werden. Das heißt, im Ernstfall wird dieser Einsatz zum Kampfeinsatz mit einem unbekannten Gegner und Ausgang. Wir sollten die Bedenken derer, die wir in den Einsatz schicken, ernst nehmen." Ibid, p. 3391.

[96] Hyde-Price 2001, p. 31.

[97] Translation by the author, original in German: „Die UNO hat die EU darum gebeten, ein Kontingent zu stellen. Auch die Afrikanische Union ist dafür. Im Kongo haben sich selbst die politisch Verantwortlichen dazu bereit erklärt, diesen Prozess zu unterstützen, damit die Demokratisierung voranschreiten kann. Dennoch führen wir – in ganz Europa nur wir – diese quälende Debatte über diesen Einsatz. In keinem anderen Land, weder in Frankreich noch sonst wo, wird eine derartige Debatte geführt." Deutscher Bundestag 2006b: Bundestag plenary protocol 16/37, p. 3252.

5.2.3 Summarising and synthesising the findings:

The decision processes and debates in the run up to and during these two instances of military interventions in Africa show that strategic culture provides an explanation for differences in the frequency and intensity with which states employ military force. The decision process was significantly shorter in the case of the British intervention to Sierra Leone. The autonomy with which the British government acted in the run-up to the intervention highlights how British strategic culture's higher proclivity to the use of force provides the necessary conditions for more frequent and robust deployment. The fact that this intervention was first debated in the House of Commons after troops were deployed highlights that justification efforts and authorisation requirements are significantly lower in the UK than in Germany. The protracted, intricate and reactive decision processes as well as the extensive debate in Germany on the other hand strongly indicate that the differences in all norms dimensions of German strategic culture established previously provide the necessary condition for Germany's restrained style of security and defence policy behaviour.

5.3 British and German military interventions in Afghanistan and elsewhere after 9/11

The terrorist attacks of 11 September 2001 were a sufficient condition for Germany and the United Kingdom to use of military force in Afghanistan. After all, both countries are close allies to the United States and members of NATO, which invoked chapter 5 of its charter for the first time shortly after 9/11. This declared the terrorist attacks on United States citizens an attack on all. The way in which the two countries used military force in Afghanistan differs. This section will attempt to trace the decision process and debates to deploy troops to Afghanistan as well as debates over deployment when the mission came under review. It will argue that British strategic culture and particularly a strong normative attachment to transatlanticism and a firm belief in the justness and utility of the resolute use of military force to pursue the goal of combating terrorism led to short, proactive decision processes, sparse debates and preferences for the resolute use of military force despite relatively high risks of own casualties. In Germany on the other hand a strong normative attachment to transatlanticism and multilateralism collided with normative reservations about the justness and utility of military force led to a longer, reactive decision process, more exhaustive debates and preferences for the restrained use of military force in the form of a concentration on civil reconstruction efforts. When the efficacy of the actions that were decided on came under review during operations in Afghanistan strategic culture impeded the endorsement of alternative options.

Because the British and German military interventions in Afghanistan are ongoing and already of very long duration this book cannot cover all debates and decisions made in the run up to and during these interventions. It will therefore first compare British and German decision processes and debates in the run up to their military involvement in Afghanistan. Then it will briefly compare two exemplary debates and decisions made when their ongoing involvement in Afghanistan became subject to a review. These are the British decision to move its ISAF forces to Helmand province in January 2006 and the German decision to allow Tornado jets to participate in aerial reconnaissance missions in March 2007.

5.3.1 The British decision to use military force following 9/11

The decision to participate in combat actions against terrorist forces and those who harbour them in Afghanistan was made within a time frame lasting from 11 September 2001 until the first day of attacks on 7 October 2001 on which the UK participated with two nuclear-powered submarines firing Tomahawk cruise missiles and with aircraft providing reconnaissance and air-to-air refuelling capabilities.[98] Reportedly, the decision was taken after two cabinet meetings which were both devoid of debate.[99] This suggests that the decision to go to war with Afghanistan centred on the Prime Minister. Indeed, Blair started preparing for and justifying the intervention from a very early point within this time frame onwards, which indicates that he took the decision to participate in Operation Enduring Freedom very shortly after 9/11. Blair's preparations for the invasion consisted of two main elements. With the shuttle diplomacy he embarked on from 19 September onwards he rallied support for the forthcoming invasion of Afghanistan. Crucially, Blair visited the Russian President Vladimir Putin and Pakistan's President, General Pervez Musharraf in order to gain their approval of a forthcoming invasion of Afghanistan. This ensured that Russia would not stand in the way of coalition forces using military bases in Central Asia and that Pakistan would not stand in the way of combat actions against Al Qaeda and the Taliban. His diplomatic efforts also included a phone conversation with then-Iranian President Mohammed Khatami, which ensured his approval, too.[100] The second element was the compilation of a government dossier titled "Responsibility for the Terrorist Atrocities in the United States"[101]. This document claimed Al Quaeda's responsibility but crucially also implicated the Taliban in the terrorist attacks.[102] This provided the basis of justifications for the invasion of Afghanistan on grounds of self-defence.

There were two debates in the House of Commons between 9/11 and the launch of OEF. Both debates bore very little disagreement and hardly put into question the need for military action. On 14 September Blair already made clear that the UK will take military action and already suggested that this action will be directed against terrorist organisations as well as states harbouring them:

> We know that these groups are fanatics, capable of killing without discrimination. ... We know, that they would, if they could, go further and use chemical, biological, or even nuclear weapons of mass destruction. We know, also, that there are groups of people, occasionally states, who will trade the technology and capability of such weapons. It is time that this trade was exposed, disrupted, and stamped out. We have been warned by the events of 11 September, and we should act on the warning.[103]

Blair justified the use of force on a broad range of grounds, ranging from self-defence by mentioning that many British citizens died as a result of the attacks to pledges of unequivocal solidarity with the United States, NATO's invocation of Article 5[104] and the defence of basic values and beliefs more generally. He ended his speech with a strong martial connotation:

> We believe in reason, democracy and tolerance. These beliefs are the foundation of our civilised world. They are enduring, they have served us well, and as history has shown, we have been prepared to fight, when necessary, to defend them. The fanatics should know that we hold our beliefs every bit as

[98] British Ministry of Defence 2007a: "Operations in Afghanistan: Background Briefing 1", 10/10/07, www.mod.uk/DefenceInternet/FactSheets/OperationsFactsheets/OperationsInAfghanistanBackgroundBriefing1

[99] Kampfner 2003, p. 129; MacAskill, Ewan/White, Michael 2001: "Bold Blair takes the zealous road to war", *The Guardian*, 29/09/2001, http://www.guardian.co.uk/waronterror/story/0,1361,560224,00.html; Williams 2005, p. 50.

[100] Kampfner 2003, pp. 119 – 128; MacAskill/White 2001; Williams 2005, p. 49.

[101] This document is available online at http://www.pm.gov.uk/output/Page3682.asp.

[102] Williams 2005, p. 49.

[103] House of Commons 2001a: Debates, *Hansard*, 14/09/2001, Volume 372, Column 604, http://www.publications.parliament.uk/pa/cm200102/cmhansrd/vo010914/debindx/10914-x.htm

[104] Article 5 of the North Atlantic Treaty states that an attack against one member state is an attack against all.

strongly as they hold theirs, and now is the time to show it.[105]

The opposition largely echoed his statement. Its leader, Iain Duncan Smith, stated:

> "I have absolutely no hesitation in giving the Prime Minister my party's full support for his immediate pledge to stand shoulder to shoulder with our strongest friends and allies in the United States. Together, we must ensure that the perpetrators are hunted down and brought to justice, as he said. … I assure him that he will have our total backing throughout in maintaining his position of unflinching support for the United States in its search for the perpetrators and its subsequent actions. … We now have an opportunity to support the United States in the defence of freedom and democracy, as it has supported us in the past."

He continued: "The message needs to go out loud and clear: those Governments who harbour terrorists will have to learn to live with the consequences of their actions."[106] The leader of the Liberal Democrats, Charles Kennedy, concurred that "It seems almost inevitable that there will be some sort of military response at some point – although at the moment we do not know where, when, or against whom." Yet he also expressed the need for moderation:

> "That said, may I strike a note of caution? American sources are indicating that NATO bombings may occur in Sudan, Iraq, Iran, Syria and Afghanistan. The whole Middle East could become a tinder box if we are not careful. I urge my right hon. Friend to talk to President Bush and to find the right targets and culprits. Ultimately, we must act not out of revenge, but out of a sense of justice."[107]

This shows that three days after 9/11, before it was even clear who was to be targeted, there was a consensus in the House of Commons that there is a need for military action.

The second time that parliament convened since 9/11 on 4 October 2001 plans for military action already crystallised. Blair informed the House that there is evidence of Osama bin Laden and Al Qaeda having planned and carried out the atrocities and of the Taliban regime in Afghanistan providing the necessary means of a safe haven for them.[108] He continued:

> "In the face of this evidence, our immediate objectives are clear. We must bring bin Laden and other al-Qaeda leaders to justice and eliminate the terrorist threat that they pose, and we must ensure that Afghanistan ceases to harbour and sustain international terrorism. If the Taliban regime will not comply with that objective, we must bring about change in that regime to ensure that Afghanistan's links to international terrorism are broken. … I can confirm that we have had initial discussions with the United States about a range of military capabilities with which Britain can help and have already responded positively."[109]

Blair moderated the bellicose keynotes of his statement by concluding that the Afghan people are not the enemy but will have his sympathy and support. He declared al-Qaeda as the enemy and added that the Taliban must yield them up or become an enemy, too.

The opposition, as expected, fully concurred. Iain Duncan Smith remarked:

> "The right hon. Gentleman has shared with me more than he is able to present here today and on that basis I am convinced that Osama bin Laden, al-Qaeda and the Taliban are guilty as charged. Any war against these people is a just war. We must stand ready to fight for our democracy and for civilised values everywhere."[110]

There was thus very little disagreement with the government's plans to fight a war in Afghanistan alongside coalition forces. Some MPs stressed the need for UN authorisation. The Foreign Secretary reasoned in response that UN Security Council resolution 1368 invokes chapter VII against terrorists as well as those who harbour them.[111] Other MPs stressed that the humanitarian needs of the Afghan people must be taken care of, especially in light of the

---

[105] House of Commons 2001a: Debates, *Hansard*, 14/09/2001, columns 606 – 607.
[106] Ibid, column 607.
[107] Ibid, column 610.
[108] House of Commons 2001b: Debates, *Hansard*, 04/10/2001, Volume 372, Column 672, http://www.publications.parliament.uk/pa/cm200102/cmhansrd/vo011004/debindx/11004-x.htm.
[109] Ibid, column 673.
[110] House of Commons 2001b: Debates, *Hansard*, 04/10/2001, Column 676.
[111] Ibid, columns 689 – 691.

forthcoming winter. Still others stressed that Afghanistan must not be abandoned once the ruling Taliban is removed from power. But there was virtually no question about the necessity of military force.

On 8 October Blair informed the House that

> "At 5.30pm British time yesterday a series of air and cruise missile attacks began on the terrorist camps of Osama bin Laden and the military installations of the Taliban regime. These were carried out by American and British armed forces with the support of other allies. There were 30 targets. ... In all cases, the utmost care was taken to avoid civilian casualties."[112]

This concluded the debate on the use of force against the Taliban and Al Qaeda in Afghanistan. The debate followed a pattern in British debates on the use of force. It was marked by a broad consensus over the justness and the necessity of the use of force, showed a preference for its robust use and allowed the government to make decisions and take actions relatively autonomously. The little controversy in the debates shows that there is less need to debate the use of force in the UK due to norms generating collective expectations of a robust military response. The British contribution to the war in Afghanistan consisted of three submarines, a military base in Diego Garcia, airpower, intelligence, Special Forces and 4000 ground troops to support US-led operations.[113] British strategic culture was a necessary condition for the intensity of the UK's use of military force in Afghanistan since 2001.

---

[112] House of Commons 2001c: Debates, *Hansard*, 08/10/2001, Volume 372, Column 811, http://www.publications.parliament.uk/pa/cm200102/cmhansrd/vo011008/debindx/11008-x.htm

[113] Williams 2005, p. 50; Ministry of Defence 2007.

5.3.2 The German decision to participate in OEF in response to 9/11

Germany's immediate response to 9/11 did not differ substantially from the UK's. Chancellor Schröder expressed Germany's unconfined solidarity immediately after the terrorist attacks.[114] All fractions in the Bundestag subsequently backed this declaration of unequivocal solidarity except for the PDS with 565 out of a total 611 possible votes.[115] The German government also supported NATO's invocation of Article 5.[116] On 11 October Schröder stated in the *Bundestag* that Germany was obliged to participate in military operations.[117] These pledges did however not translate into active support for an immediate military response to 9/11. Longhurst argues: "Crucially, at both elite and societal levels reticence on the use of force and fear of US unilateralism pervaded the German debate".[118] Schröders proclamations were met with unease by many in the public, the Greens and even the SPD as there were fears that the US would overreact and respond unilaterally, which could have uncontrollable consequences such as an escalation of the conflict over the wider Middle East. A war against terrorism involving civilian deaths would therefore be the exact wrong way to respond.[119] The German government pursued its traditional preference for a multilateral approach aimed at tackling terrorism through diplomatic as well as restrained military means. Germany's preferences for political and diplomatic means are demonstrated by Fischer's efforts to forge a common diplomatic response in the EU, to embolden the UN and to revive the dialogue between Israelis and Palestinians, although ultimately unsuccessful, as well as Germany's facilitation of the UN-sponsored conference in Bonn on the construction of a post-Taliban regime in late November.[120] Already at this point one can discern that Germany's immediate reaction to 9/11 differed sharply to the UK's because norms contained in German strategic culture generated public expectations which led to different preferences of German decision-makers to pursue their goal of helping the US to combat terrorism. These preferences were to ensure the US their loyalty whilst pursuing non-military means to combat terrorism. When the US made explicit demands for a military contribution in early November decision-makers were caught in between normative attachments to its allies and partners and strong domestic normative reservations over the use of force. Germans were understanding of the US-led war in Afghanistan but sceptical of its adequacy. Scott Erb argues: "early German support was reminiscent of the Gulf War, albeit with fewer protests".[121] And indeed, this duality of normative attachments to Germany's allies and normative reservations about the justness and efficacy of military force is a recurring pattern in German foreign, defence and security policy since the end of the Cold War.

Schröder's pledge to a military contribution in Afghanistan thus met in part with staunch domestic opposition generally and within the red-green coalition.[122] After the cabinet drafted a motion on 6 November to make 3900 troops available numerous members of the SPD and the Greens expressed their intention to vote against it.[123] To ensure parliamentary approval,

[114] „Ich habe ihm [George Bush] auch die uneingeschränkte, ich betone: die uneingeschränkte Solidarität Deutschlands zugesichert.", Deutscher Bundestag 2001a: Plenary Protocol 14/186, 12/11/2001, p. 18293, http://dip.bundestag.de/btp/14/14186.pdf

[115] Bundestag 2001b: Plenary Protocol 14/187, 19/11/2001, p. 18337, http://dip.bundestag.de/btp/14/14187.pdf

[116] Longhurst 2004, p. 82; Erb, Scott 2003: "German Foreign Policy: Navigating a New Era", Lynne Rienner, Boulder CO, p. 193.

[117] Bundestag 2001c: Plenary Protocol 14/192, 11/10/2001, p. 18682, http://dip.bundestag.de/btp/14/14192.pdf.

[118] Longhurst 2004, pp. 82 – 83.

[119] Ibid, p. 83; Erb 2003, pp. 193 – 194.8

[120] Longhurst 2004, p. 83; Erb 2003, p. 193.

[121] Erb 2003, p. 194 – 195.

[122] Longhurst 2004, pp. 83 – 84; Erb 2003, pp. 194 – 196.

[123] Longhurst 2004, p. 84; Erb 2003, p. 195; „Dem Kanzler droht der Verlust der eigenen Mehrheit", *Frankfurter Allgemeine Zeitung*, 12/11/2001, p. 1.

Schröder was not content to rely on the opposition's support to compensate for lack of support from within his own coalition, as it was the case when the *Bundestag* decided on Germany's participation in Operation Essential Harvest on 29 August 2001. As the number of opponents to the proposal rose even within the SPD Schröder resorted to the rare and compelling means of coupling the vote on a *Bundeswehr* participation in OEF to a vote of confidence or *Vertrauensfrage*.[124] This means was only used three times in the Federal Republic's history. It tied the decision to deploy troops to the coalition government's continued existence and thereby made it vastly more intricate. On 16 November 2001 the *Bundestag* voted for a German participation in OEF with a maximum of 3900 troops by 336 votes for and 326 against. By this time Kabul had already fallen to the Northern Alliance and other Taliban strongholds were weakening. The decision therefore already lost its relevance in large parts since the US-led invasion of Afghanistan has already progressed far by then.[125] Ultimately, the bulk of the envisaged 3900 troops were not deployed to Afghanistan but to the Horn of Africa to patrol and monitor shipping routes.

This protracted, reactive decision process is characteristic of German decisions to use force. It shows that norms contained in German strategic culture render large parts of the German public and its foreign, security and defence policy elites more sceptical of the morality of war as a means to achieve one's security and defence policy goals. This decision process was once again marked by a constellation of tensions between collective expectations stemming from the first and those stemming from the third norm category discussed in chapter 3 as well as a constellation of tensions between domestic and international demands. It also shows that heads of government are not expected to act as autonomously as in the UK and they are expected to use force with utmost restraint. This generated preferences for emphasising non-military diplomatic and political means until it became necessary to decide, in response to international demands, to use military force.

The quality and quantity of German parliamentary debates on the use of military force against terrorism also differed sharply from the UK's. This indicates that there is more need for debates on the use of force as it is an infinitely more controversial matter in Germany than in the UK. One indication for this is that those who supported a German participation in OEF used the term war (*Krieg*) only in the context of a war against the US and the civilised world but avoided speaking of a war against terrorism. The statements in the *Bundestag* on 12 September there were several references to a declaration of war but none to an active participation in a war.[126] In the second debate since 9/11 on 19 September the term *Krieg* did not appear a single time in the context of a war against terrorism. Schröder emphasised that Germany was not at war against a particular state or against the Islamic world but that terrorists declared this war upon it and must be brought to justice.[127] Unease with the term war was also present amongst members of the opposition. The CDU parliamentarian Wolfgang Freiherr von Stetten commented on his vote for the declaration:

> "Despite all the horror of this terrorist atrocity one must soberly realise: we are not at war. America has our complete solidarity ... But there must be no automatism for the *Bundeswehr* to military interventions decided upon by the US."[128]

Seemingly, parliamentarians in favour of a German participation in OEF avoided the implication that Germany would then actively be involved in fighting a war whereas those who op-

[124] Erb 2003, p. 196.

[125] Erb 2003, pp. 196 – 197, Longhurst 2004, pp. 86.

[126] Bundestag 2001a: Plenary Protocol 14/186, 12/11/2001.

[127] Bundestag 2001b: Plenary Protocol 14/187, 19/11/2001, p. 18303.

[128] Translation by the author, original in German: „Bei allem Erschrecken über den Terroranschlag muss man nüchtern feststellen: Wir befinden uns nicht im Krieg. Amerika gehört unsere volle Solidarität ... Es kann aber keinen Automatismus für von den USA getroffene militärische Einsätze für die Bundeswehr geben". Ibid, p. 18342.

posed a German participation used the term war with great frequency. German sensitivities towards the term "war" can be discerned in the following interjections by SPD parliamentarians during a speech by the PDS parliamentarian Roland Claus on 16 November:

> „‚Sie sind der erste Bundeskanzler, der diese Vertrauensfrage und damit sein Schicksal mit einer Zustimmung zu Kriegseinsätzen verbindet.'
> (Dr. Peter Struck [SPD]: **‚‚Kriegseinsätze'! Hören Sie auf damit!'**)
> ‚Wir bleiben dabei: Die PDS-Fraktion sagt Nein zu diesem Krieg, Nein zur deutschen Beteiligung und auch Nein zur Vertrauensfrage.'
> (Beifall bei der PDS. Lothar Mark [SPD]: ‚**Deutschland beteiligt sich nicht am Krieg!'**)"[129]

The language used in German debates on the use of force strongly contrasts with the British discourse. After all, it is hard to imagine hearing phrases such as "any war against these people is a just war" in the *Bundestag*.

The debate before the vote of confidence on 16 November highlighted a number of other complexities of German strategic culture. With a single vote *Bundestag* members had to decide on the use of force and the continued existence of the red-green coalition government. Those within the SPD and the Greens opposed to the government's proposal complained that this challenged their right to vote their conscience. Schröder justified the *Vertrauensfrage* and the planned deployment on the same grounds. He argued that the government must maintain Germany's credibility as a reliable ally. Soon-to-be defence minister Peter Struck added that military means were only one amongst many other at least equally important non-military means employed by the government and that only by committing troops now can Germany have a stake in post-war reconstruction efforts. He added that "Art und Umfang des jetzt zugesagten militärischen Beistandes sind bei allen generellen Bedenken gegen militärische Einsätze verantwortbar und leistbar." Referring to a twelve-page article that appeared in the magazine *Stern* the day before this debate in which a number of well known German intellectuals demanded the government to "stop this war"[130], Struck specified Germany's military contribution to OEF. Aside from paramedics, logistical support, precautionary deployment of NBC detection troops to Kuwait and marines to monitor and ensure the safety of civilian shipping routes Germany would deploy 100 of its Special Forces, the *Kommandospezialkräfte* (KSK) to Afghanistan. Their tasks were continuously portrayed as "police-like".[131] The opposition CDU/CSU and FDP fractions, which both supported deployment, instead criticised the government more generally of being unfit to govern. Kerstin Müller from the Greens argued that the government's specification of the mandate and the chancellor's assurances that German soldiers will neither participate in air strikes nor in combat missions on the ground moved many Greens to support the motion.[132] Nevertheless, over seventy members of parliament who supported the motion stated in written explanations of their vote that they only gave their support to keep the coalition in power but still objected military deployment.[133]

---

[129] Emphasis added. Author's translation: "'You are the first Federal Chancellor who links this vote of confidence and thereby his fortunes with an approval to a war operation (*Kriegseinsatz)*.' (Dr. Peter Struck [SPD]: **war operation! Just stop it!**) 'We maintain: The PDS faction says no to this war, no to a German participation and no to the vote of confidence.' (Applause from the PDS. Lothar Mark [SPD]: **"Germany does not participate in war!"**) Bundestag 2001d: Plenary Protocol 14/202, 16/11/2001, p. 19870, http://dip.bundestag.de/btp/14/14202.pdf, emphasis added.

[130] „Aufruf gegen den Krieg", *Stern*, 15/11/2001, pp. 54 – 70. This article in itself indicates that there were collective expectations of the government not to go to war with Afghanistan generated by distinctly anti-militaristic norms.

[131] The limitation of the KSK's mandate to quasi police-military tasks was mentioned nine times during the debate. See Bundestag 2001d: Plenary Protocol 14/202, 16/11/2001, pp. 19863, 19868, 19872, 19888, 19900, 19901, 19904, 19905, and 19908.

[132] „Der Bundeskanzler hat außerdem klar gestellt, dass sich deutsche Soldaten weder an Luftangriffen noch an Kampftruppen am Boden beteiligen werden." Bundestag 2001d: Plenary Protocol 14/202, 16/11/2001, p. 19868.

[133] Longhurst 2004, p. 86.

The German debate on the use of force in response to 9/11 fits into a pattern of German debates on the use of force. It was a protracted and complex debate in which the morality of war as a means for achieving political ends stood against loyalty to Germany's allies. The latter once again played an important role in justifications of the use of force. It exposed a strong preference to use force restrictively and to avoid combat situations and casualties as much as possible. In short, it showed that Germany intervenes less frequently and intensely because its military contributions are a compromise between norms generating collective expectations of alliance solidarity (*Bündnissolidarität*) and norms generating collective expectations of Germany not to participate in combat missions (*Kampfeinsätze*).

5.3.3 British and German decisions in response to reviews of military interventions in Afghanistan

By the end of 2001 the Taliban fell from power in Afghanistan. The Bonn Agreement passed on 5 December 2001 at the end of the UN-sponsored conference in Bonn raised the idea of a NATO-led International Security Assistance Force (ISAF) to secure peace and stability in post-war Afghanistan. After the UK government hosted a conference on potential troop contributions Foreign Secretary Jack Straw offered the UN to take the first lead of ISAF on 19 December.[134] The next day UN Security Council Resolution 1386 authorised this mission. The *Bundestag* decided on a German participation in ISAF on 22 December. Although the mission was originally confined to Kabul it gradually expanded into other provinces in the form of Provincial Reconstruction Teams (PRTs). By autumn 2004 there were 19 PRTs throughout the country. The UK led two PRTs in Meymaneh and Mazar-e-Sharif and Germany established PRTs in Kunduz and Feizabad.[135] Ensuring peace and stability in Afghanistan soon turned out to be an arduous task in the face of ongoing attacks by remaining Al Qaeda and Taliban fighters. While ISAF did have a somewhat positive impact upon the security situation in Kabul, warlordism, heroin production and banditry were rampant in the rest of the country, especially its south and southeast. This led to the gradual emergence of a review process amongst ISAF contributing nations. Judging by previous findings about British and German strategic culture one would expect Germany to continue to focus on civilian reconstruction efforts while the UK would opt for more military means for the common goal of ensuring stability. Table 14 suggests that the respective strategic cultures would provide the necessary conditions for such preferences because in contrast to British respondents the majority of Germans disapproves of the *Bundeswehr* participating in combat operations in Afghanistan.

Table 14: " To what extent, would you approve or disapprove of the deployment of (British/German) troops for the following operations?" (responses in %)

a) To contribute to international reconstruction efforts in Afghanistan.

	Approve very much	Approve somewhat	Disapprove somewhat	Disapprove very much	Don't know/refusal
Germany	20	38	23	18	1
UK	28	41	14	13	5

b) To conduct combat operations against the Taliban in Afghanistan.

	Approve very much	Approve somewhat	Disapprove somewhat	Disapprove very much	Don't know/refusal
Germany	9	15	33	42	1
UK	19	32	24	20	6

Source: Transatlantic Trends 2007, pp. 32 – 33.

At a NATO summit in Brussels on 8 December 2005 the alliance's foreign ministers endorsed a plan to expand ISAF's role and presence in Afghanistan. The first element of this plan was to expand ISAF into the south of the country, the third stage of its expansion. This plan envis-

[134] Williams 2005, p. 53.

[135] Ibid, p. 55; Most information on German military involvement in Afghanistan within ISAF is taken from the official *Bundeswehr* website at www.einsatz.bundeswehr.de.

aged British troops to move into Helmand province.[136] PRTs in Meymaneh and Mazar-e-Sharif would be handed over to Swedish and Norwegian responsibility and new PRTs would be established in Lashkar Gar, the capital of Helmand province.[137] While it was not possible to obtain information on the details of the decision process at the NATO summit it is highly likely that the British foreign minister was fully aware that the implementation of this plan would involve engagements with Taliban and Al Qaeda forces. On 26 January 2006 British Defence Secretary John Reid announced to the members of the House of Commons that a "Helmand taskforce" consisting of a 3300 soldiers strong battle group and several newly acquired attack helicopters will be deployed to southern Afghanistan "to provide the security framework" for the envisaged provincial reconstruction team by July 2006. Reid added that "we are deploying this potent force to protect and deter. The ISAF mission is unchanged. It is focused on reconstruction." He added that as opposed to tasks for OEF Helmand taskforce would not adopt a primarily counter-terrorist role. Nevertheless it would respond robustly to insurgencies and attacks. Highlighting the high risks involved in this mission he stated that

> "Southern Afghanistan is undeniably a more demanding area in which to operate than either the north or the west. The Taliban remains active. The authority of the Afghan Government—and the reach of their security forces—is still weak. The influence of the drugs traffickers, by contrast, is strong."[138]

While the House shared his concern over the grave risks involved in his plans and several warned of overstretch of the British armed forces in the light of its engagements in Iraq most of its members were generally supportive of Reid's plans. It should be noted however, that although Reid made a copy of his statement available to the opposition in advance he made the decision to deploy troops to the south of Afghanistan before making this statement before the House of Commons. The UK's Ministry of Defence states on its website:

> "The UK's deployment to Helmand has seen several small and medium-size operations designed to root out insurgents. These are an essential prelude to implementing the main, unchanged, ISAF mission: facilitating reconstruction and the extension of government authority."[139]

Once again, as in many other British decisions to use force, the decision process was short, parliamentary debates were virtually non-existent prior to the decision and fighting, as it turned out, was intense. This all shows that British strategic culture's proclivity to the use of force provided the necessary condition for the British decision to deploy troops to the south of Afghanistan in January 2006.

German strategic culture's relatively low proclivity to the use of force on the other hand provided the necessary condition for the continuation of restrained military behaviour despite a review of its engagement in Afghanistan. Germany most likely pursued the preferences hypothesised on the basis of Table 14 at the NATO summit in Brussels on 8 December 2005. Rather than moving south Germany became the lead nation of ISAF's Region North, which included the two PRTs handed over by Britain to Norway and Sweden as well as the two German PRTs and a Hungarian PRT in Pol-e-Khomri.[140] As NATO troops deployed in the south of Afghanistan faced an increasingly hostile environment which compelled local ISAF forces to engage in hazardous anti-terrorist operations voices within NATO demanding a more active German contribution to the fight against terrorism in Afghanistan grew louder. This led to severe altercations especially with Germany's American, British and Canadian

[136] NATO 2007: "International Security Assistance Force (ISAF) – How did this operation evolve?", 24/07/2007, http://www.nato.int/issues/isaf/evolution.html.

[137] British Ministry of Defence 2007: "Operations in Afghanistan: Background Briefing 1", 10/10/07, www.mod.uk/DefenceInternet/FactSheets/OperationsFactsheets/OperationsInAfghanistanBackgroundBriefing1

[138] House of Commons 2006: Debates, *Hansard*, 26/01/06, Volume 126, Column 1530, http://www.publications.parliament.uk/pa/cm200506/cmhansrd/vo060126/debtext/60126-11.htm

[139] British Ministry of Defence 2007: "Operations in Afghanistan: Background Briefing 1".

[140] Bundeswehr 2007: "Breites Leistungsspektrum: Die Bundeswehr in Afghanistan", 12/09/2007, www.bundeswehr.de

NATO partners.[141] Yet the *Bundestag* equipped German ISAF soldiers with a restrictive mandate that does not permit German soldiers to engage in combat activities exceeding their individual and collective right to self-defence outside their area of responsibility. NATO General Secretary Jaap de Hoop Scheffer announced on 26 January 2007 at a meeting of the North Atlantic Council that he would appreciate a German participation in aerial reconnaissance missions as NATO lacks of surveillance planes in Afghanistan. This sparked a long and protracted decision process and debate in Germany.[142] After the government decided that such aerial reconnaissance was not covered by the existing mandate it tabled a motion to allow Tornado jets to participate in aerial reconnaissance missions.[143] However, voices of dissent soon emerged, even within parts of the governing grand coalition itself. The CDU parliamentarian Willy Wimmer for instance reportedly argued that „The German pilots, who, with these planes, identify those villages, which are subsequently destroyed by the Americans, are thereby on a direct flight to The Hague".[144] On 6 February a group called Organisation of International Doctors for the Prevention of a Nuclear War sent a letter of protest to the cabinet in which it claimed that an opinion survey revealed that 77 percent of Germans reject a German participation in aerial reconnaissance missions.[145] On 28 February the *Bundestag* discussed the governments motion for the first time to decide on its referral to the *Bundestag*'s foreign affairs committee for primary consultation and to its defence committee, its judiciary committee, its committee for human rights and humanitarian aid, its committee for economic cooperation and development and the budgetary committee for additional consultation.[146] After these committees recommended the approval of the government's motion on 7 March 2007[147] the final parliamentary debate took place on 9 March. This debate was marked by the proponent's usual arguments stressing the importance of *Bündnissolidarität* and the importance of ISAF for Germany's security as well as strict avoidance of the term *Kampfeinsatz*. Opponents argued that the *Bundeswehr* was getting increasingly drawn into OEF tasks and combat operations not conform to its mandate.[148] With 405 votes for, 157 against and 11 abstentions the *Bundestag* adopted the government's motion. Against the motion voted five members of the CDU, 69 members of the SPD, nine members of the FDP, 21 Green parliamentarians and the entire Left fraction.[149] This demonstrates the controversial nature of this decision. Another indication for deep German sensitivities are two expedited motions which two CDU parliamentarians and the Left fraction respectively passed to the German constitutional court. The court rejected these motions on 12 March and 29 March respectively.[150] After this enormous parliamentary scrutiny the Tornado jets first took off on 15 April 2007. It

---

[141] Gebauer, Matthias/Weiland, Severin 2007: „USA und Briten überziehen Deutschland mit Kritik Kampagne", *Spiegel Online*, 17/11/2006, http://www.spiegel.de/politik/deutschland/0,1518,449160,00.html

[142] Weiland, Severin 2007: „Tornados in Startposition", *Spiegel Online*, 26/01/2007, http://www.spiegel.de/politik/deutschland/0,1518,462492,00.html.

[143] Deutscher Bundestag 2007: Drucksache 16/4298, 08/02/2007, http://dip21.bundestag.de/dip21/btd/16/042/1604298.pdf

[144] Translation by the author, original in German: „Die deutschen Piloten, die mit diesen Flugzeugen die Dörfer ausfindig machen, die anschließend von den Amerikanern zerstört werden, sind damit auf dem direkten Flug nach Den Haag". Weiland 2007.

[145] http://www.spiegel.de/politik/deutschland/0,1518,464566,00.html

[146] Deutscher Bundestag: Plenary Protocol 16/81, 28/01/2007, pp. 8127, 8144, document available online at http://dip21.bundestag.de/dip21/btp/16/16081.pdf.

[147] Deutscher Bundestag: Printed paper 16/4571, 07/03/2007, http://dip21.bundestag.de/dip21/btd/16/045/1604571.pdf; Deutscher Bundestag: Printed paper 16/4580, 07/03/2007, http://dip21.bundestag.de/dip21/btd/16/045/1604580.pdf.

[148] Deutscher Bundestag: Plenary protocol 16/86, 09/03/2007, http://dip21.bundestag.de/dip21/btp/16/16086.pdf.

[149] Ibid, pp. 8713 – 8714.

[150] „Verfassungsgericht lehnt Eilantrag ab", *Stern.de*, 30/03/2007, http://www.stern.de/politik/deutschland/585957.html?nv=ct_mt; Luftwaffe 2007: „Entscheidung über Aufklärungsflüge der Luftwaffe", 03/07/2007, News archive of the official website of the German air force, available online at www.luftwaffe.de.

is remarkable how fundamentally decision processes and debates on the use of force differ in Germany and the United Kingdom.

5.3.4 Summarising and synthesising the findings

The UK first used military force against Afghanistan on 8 October 2001. Since then the UK continuously used military force on the ground and from the air to fight against Taliban and Al Qaeda forces within the framework of OEF as well as ISAF. Germany first participated in OEF in January 2002. The bulk of its contribution to OEF consists of marine soldiers patrolling and monitoring shipping routes along the Horn of Africa. Germany's large-scale participation in ISAF in the north of Afghanistan focuses on civilian reconstruction efforts. It took an enormously long decision process and intense debates until the Federal Government authorised Tornado jets to perform tasks basically involving photography. This book argues that differences between German and British strategic culture provides the only viable explanation for this vast variance in military behaviour towards Afghanistan. Norms on the use of force in the UK allowed for the government to use force decisively in Afghanistan whereas norms in Germany generally caused expectations that the government would not allow its troops to engage in combat activities.

CONCLUSION

In conclusion, the findings of this book suggest that the nail comes before the hammer. The UK did not use military force more frequently and more intensively since 1990 because it has more and better capabilities to do so. The shortcoming of this neorealist explanation is that Germany and the UK are roughly equal in their potential power capabilities but they differ in the degree to which they translate potential into actual capabilities. A possible counter-argument to this critique is that Germany lacks combat experience, which precludes this translation. Yet crucially, opinion surveys as well as qualitative and quantitative comparisons of decision processes and debates on the use of force reveal that in Germany there is significantly less political will in significantly more circumstances to engage in combat activity, let alone to acquire combat experience. The public and political elites in Germany consciously take into account the discrepancy between potential and actual military power in Germany. This shows that culturally derived norms, ideas and beliefs about the use of military force rather than a state's military capabilities determine its behaviour regarding the use of military force.

In chapter 3 the author argued that British strategic culture entails a higher proclivity to use force in four dimensions of norms on the use of force. In theory, these norms should generate collective expectations more in line with a world power, or at least junior world power, identity and thereby allow actors to assign options involving the relatively extensive use of force a comparatively high position in ranked sets of options to pursue its security and defence policy goals. For Germany on the other hand, the findings in chapter 3 suggest that strategic culture should generate collective expectations in line with a civilian power identity. This should entail actors to assign the use of force a comparatively lower position in ranked sets of options to pursue its security and defence policy goals.

Chapter 4 established a positive correlation between variations found in norms concerning the use of force contained in strategic culture through opinion polls on the one hand and variations in the frequency and intensity of the use of military force found through a combined mission and head count as well as an analysis of each deployment's mandate on the other hand.

Chapter 5 traced the decision processes and briefly analysed debates in the run up to four instances of military interventions abroad and during a review process of the military interventions in Kosovo and Afghanistan. It found that in each instance decision processes and parliamentary debates led to different sets of preference rankings. In Germany protracted and reactive decision processes as well as exhaustive debates indicated expectations of and preferences for non-military means to be used first, high restrictions to be imposed upon mandates, extensive domestic and international authorisation requirements to be adhered to and actions to be closely coordinated with allies and partners within multilateral frameworks. This led to decisions to employ military force less intensively and frequently. In the UK on the other hand decisions were made within shorter time, more autonomously and more proactively. Parliamentary debates were consensual rather than controversial and did not play as important a role as German parliamentary debates did in the run up to a decision to use force. This indicates that British strategic culture causes the British public and its elites to be comparatively more at ease with the use of military force. This provides a necessary condition for decisions to employ military force more intensively and more frequently.

This book took on the task of empirically and objectively analysing the relationship between strategic culture and military behaviour. A few shortcomings must be conceded. Within the scope of this book it was not possible to take all indications of the causal processes of strategic culture into account. More exhaustive use of opinion polls, a systematic media analysis and a more exhaustive discourse analysis may have rendered further plausibility the alleged causal processes. This can be the task of future research projects.

The book also concentrated on variations across rather than within cases. It merely touched upon variations within German strategic culture across time despite the existence of a vast body of literature on this issue. Neither did this book account for variations in British strategic culture across time. There is a strong possibility that the recent invasion of Iraq and its aftermath significantly altered British norms on the use of military force. An analysis of variations within strategic cultures over time and an analysis of the mechanisms behind these variations can therefore also be the task of future research projects.

Yet despite this particular shortcoming this book can assert with relative certainty that the variation between British and German strategic cultures still cause the respective military behaviour to operate within separate margins. This challenges assertions of Germany having transitioned from a 'civilian power' to a 'normal power' identity. Although it is a matter of definition to judge such assertions the contrasts between opinion polls, decision processes and debates in Germany and the UK indicate that Germany is still a civilian power.

Another possible shortcoming may have been that this book was not always free from implicit normative judgements. Since decisions to use military force involve numerous complex moral problems and dilemmas it is hardly possible to refrain from such judgements when writing about these decisions. It may now be permitted to make these judgements explicit.

In the cases of military interventions in Kosovo, Sierra Leone and the DR Congo both countries were willing to deploy troops for humanitarian purposes. Yet especially the example of the British intervention in Sierra Leone showed that British strategic culture allows it to intervene more robustly since it does not treat humanitarian interventions as controversially as German strategic culture does. Decisions to use force for humanitarian purposes require actors to choose between two different schools of moral philosophy. German decision-makers seem to take more of a Kantian approach whereas British actors seem to base their judgements more on Utilitarian grounds. While both positions are based on profound philosophical reflections the example of Sierra Leone highlights that military force, if used effectively, can put an end to horrific civil wars and vicious crimes against humanity.

The difference between the German and British response to the terrorist attacks of 11 September 2001 suggests that British and German strategic culture entail two different approaches to international order. In Germany many argued that fighting terrorism with military means is counterproductive whereas the UK was very quick to employ military means against terrorism alongside the US. Edward Hallet Carr wrote in The Twenty Years' Crisis that ultimately world order rests on morality as much as on power. It cannot rest on either one alone. In neglecting the factor of power as the basis of the current order Germany risks becoming a free-rider of other powers defending the status quo against challengers. Just as order cannot rest on either power or morality alone terrorism cannot be defeated by either military or non-military means alone.

Lastly, the ESS calls for the development of a strategic culture that fosters early, rapid and, when necessary, robust intervention. In the light of the findings of this book one can argue that British strategic culture is a lot closer to this proclaimed ideal than German strategic culture. Europe's cultural diversity allows Europeans to learn from and inspire each other through knowledge about each other's cultural differences. Knowledge about the differences of each others' strategic cultures can serve the same purpose.

The main task of this book was to provide an explanation for differences in military behaviour despite similar power capabilities, a similar institutional embedding and a similar degree of democratisation. What this book can claim with relative certainty is that strategic culture can provide a viable explanation to this puzzle and that therefore strategic culture matters.

BIBLIOGRAPHY

Abrams, Fran 1998: "Blair: 'We did nothing wrong", *The Independent*, 12/05/98

Bacia, Horst 2006: „Spring Du, ich schieße", *FAZ-NET*, 15/03/2006, article available online at www.faz.net

Baldwin, David 1979: "Power Analysis and World Politics", *World Politics* 31: 2 (January), pp. 161-194

Baumann, Rainer 2001: "German Security Policy Within NATO", in: Rittberger, Volker (ed.): German Foreign Policy Since Unification, Manchester University Press, Manchester, pp. 141 - 185

BBC 1999: "Ground Troops an Option – Blair", *BBC Online Network*, 21/04/99, http://news.bbc.co.uk/2/hi/uk_news/politics/324877.stm

BBC 2007: "Where are British Troops and Why?", 02/10/07 http://news.bbc.co.uk/2/hi/uk_news/4094818.stm

Bellamy, Alex J. 2002: "Kosovo and International Society", Palgrave MacMillan, Basingstoke

Bellamy, Christopher 1995: "UK Forces Angola-bound" *The Independent* 14/04/95.

Bertelsmann Foundation 2007: "Who Rules the World?", 22/10/2007, www.bertelsmann-stiftung.de

Blair, Tony 1999: "A New Moral Crusade", *Newsweek*, 14/06/1999

British Ministry of Defence 2007a: "Operations in Afghanistan: Background Briefing 1", 10/10/07,www.mod.uk/DefenceInternet/FactSheets/OperationsFactsheets/OperationsInAfghanistanBackgroundBriefing1

British Ministry of Defence 2007b: "Operations in Iraq: Facts and Figures", 17/12/07, http://www.mod.uk/DefenceInternet/FactSheets/OperationsFactsheets/OperationsInIraqFactsandFigures.htm

Brown, Chris 2004: "Britain and the European Security Strategy", European Foreign Policy Research Network Working Paper No. 6, 08/07/04, http://fornet.info/documents/Working%20Paper%20no%206.pdf

Bundeswehr 2007b: „Chronologie der Einsätze der Bundeswehr in Bosnien-Herzegowina", 5/12/07, www.einsatz.bundeswehr.de

Carr, E. H. 1981: "The Twenty Years' Crisis", Palgrave MacMillan, New York and Basingstoke

Checkel, Jeffrey 1998: "The Constructivist Turn in International Relations Theory", *World Politics* 50:1, pp. 324 - 348

Cohen, Roger 1999: "Schroeder's Blunt 'No' to Ground Troops in Kosovo Reflects Depth of German Sensitivities", *New York Times*, 20/05/99.

Czempiel, Ernst-Otto 1981: „Internationale Politik. Ein Konfliktmodell", Schöningh, Paderborn.

Dalvi, Sameera 2003: "Germany", in: Glenn, John/Howlett, Darry/Poore, Stuart: "Neorealism versus Strategic Culture", Ashgate, Aldershot, pp. 204 – 223.

Lewis, Damien 2005: "Operation Certain Death", Century, London

Der Derian, James (ed.) 2003: "International Theory: Critical Investigations", Macmillan, London and Basingstoke.

Deutsche Bundeswehr 2007a: „Abgeschlossene Einsätze", 18/09/07, www.einsatz.bundeswehr.de.

Erb, Scott 2003: "German Foreign Policy: Navigating a New Era", Lynne Rienner, Boulder CO.

EU Directorate General Communication 2005: "Standard Eurobarometer 64", December, http://ec.europa.eu/public_opinion/index_en.htm.

Elington, James W. 1993: "Grounding for the Metaphysics of Morals", 3rd ed., Hackett, Indianapolis.
Elshtain, Jean Bethke 1995: "Feminist Themes and International Relations", in Der Derian, James (ed.): "International Theory: Critical Investigations", Macmillan, London and Basingstoke, pp.
Finnemore, Martha 2003: "The Purpose of Intervention", Cornell University Press, Ithaca and London.
Fischer, Joschka 1994: „Risiko Deutschland", Kiepenheuer & Witsch, Cologne.
Fischer, Joschka 2008: „Die Rot-Grünen Jahre: Deutsche Außenpolitik vom Kosovo bis zum 11. Dezember", Droemer Knaur, Munich.
Gebauer, Matthias/Weiland, Severin 2007: „USA und Briten überziehen Deutschland mit Kritik Kampagne", *Spiegel Online*, 17/11/2006, http://www.spiegel.de/politik/deutschland/0,1518,449160,00.html.
Geertz, Clifford 1973: "The Interpretation of Cultures", Basic Books, New York.
George, Alexander L./Bennet, Andrew 2004: "Case Studies and Theory Development in the Social Sciences", MIT Press, Cambridge MA
German Marshall Fund et al. 2005: "Transatlantic Trends", 09/2005, www.transatlantictrends.org
German Marshall Fund et al. 2006: "Transatlantic Trends", 09/2006, www.transatlantictrends.org
German Marshall Fund et al. 2007: "Transatlantic Trends", 09/2007, www.transatlantictrends.org
Glenn, John/Howlett, Darry/Poore, Stuart 2003: "Neorealism versus Strategic Culture", Ashgate, Aldershot.
Gray, Colin S. 1999a: "Modern Strategy", Oxford University Press, New York and Oxford, 1999
Gray, Colin S. 1999b: "Strategic Culture as Context: the First Generation of Theory Strikes Back", *Review of International Studies* 25, 49 - 69
Guthrie, General Sir Charles 200, "Bringing the Armed Forces into a New Millenium", *Royal Defence Institute Journal* (February), pp. 1 - 8
Hellmann, Gunther et al. 2005: „Deutsche Außenpolitik", VS Verlag, Frankfurt am Main
Hoon, Geoffrey 2000: "Kosovo: One Year After", *Journal of the Royal United Services Institute* (April),
Hurd, Douglas 1997: "The Search for Peace", Little, Brown, London.
Hyde-Price, Adrian 2001: "Germany and the Kosovo War", *German Politics* 10:1 (April), pp. 19 – 34.
Howard, Michael 1978: "The Forgotten Dimensions of Strategy", *Foreign Affairs* 57: 5 (winter), pp. 975 - 986
ICRC 2007: "People On War 2007 Country Report: Great Britain", 12/12/07, www.icrc.org
Inglehart et al. 2006: "World Values Survey", www.worldvaluessurvey.com
Jenkins, Simon 2000: "Stuck in the mire of the white man's burden", *The Times*, 10/05/2000
Johnson, James 1991: „Habermas on Strategic and Communicative Action", *Political Theory* 19:2 (May), pp. 181 - 201
Johnston, Iain 1995a: "Cultural Realism - Strategic Culture and Grand Strategy in Chinese History", Princeton: Princeton University Press
Johnston, Iain 1995b: "Thinking about Strategic Culture", *International Security* 19:4 (Spring 1995), pp. 32 – 64.
Judah, Tim 2000: "Kosovo: War and Revenge", Yale University Press, New Haven and London
Kaiser, Karl/Becher, Klaus 1992: "Deutschland und der Irak Konflikt: Internationale Sicherheitsverantwortung Deutschlands und Europas nach der deutschen Vereinigung",

Arbeitspapiere zur Internationalen Politik 68 (February), DGAP, Bonn, pp. 47 - 52
Kargbo, Michael 2006: "British Foreign Policy in Sierra Leone", Peter Lang, Bern
Kampfner, John 2003: "Blair's Wars", Simon & Schuster, London
Kant, Immanuel 1795: "Zum ewigen Frieden: Ein philosophischer Entwurf", in: Höffe, Ottfried (ed.) 2004: „Immanuel Kant, zum ewigen Frieden, Akademie, Berlin
Katzenstein, Peter J. (ed.) 1996: "The Culture of National Security: Norms and Identity in World Politics", Columbia University Press, New York.
Katzenstein, Peter J. 1998: "Cultural Norms and National Security: Police and Military in Postwar Japan", Cornell University Press, Ithaca and London
Keen, David 2007: "Labour's love's lost", *Le Monde Diplomatique* (May), http://mondediplo.com/2007/05/18labour.
Kohl, Helmut 2005: "Erinnerungen, 1982 – 1990", Drömer Verlag, Munich.
Krause, Joachim 2000: "Deutschland und die Kosovo-Krise", in: Reuter, Jens/Clewing, Conrad (ed.) 2000: "Der Kosovo Konflikt. Ursachen, Verlauf, Perspektiven", Wieser Verlag, Klagenfurt.
Lantis, Jeffrey 2002: "Strategic Culture and National Security Policy" International Studies Review 4: 3, pp. 87 – 113.
Longhurst, Kerry 2004: "Germany and the use of force", Manchester University Press, Manchester.
Lynch, Colum 2000a: "UN Force Crumbles In Sierra Leone, Peacekeepers Begin Surrender to Rebels", *Washington Post*, 06/05/2000, p. 1.
Lynch, Colum 2000b: "Rebels Advance Toward Freetown, Reports Differ on UN Clashes With Sierra Leone Insurgents", *Washington Post*, 07/05/2000, p. 1
Major, John 1999: "The Autobiography", HarperCollins, London.
Mangold, Peter 2001: "Success and Failure in British Foreign Policy", Palgrave, Basingstoke
Mannigart, Phillippe et al. 2001: "Europeans and a Common Security and Defense Policy: Technical Report (Tables)", Royal Military Academy, Brussels.
MacAskill, Ewan/Norton-Taylor, Richard 2000: "Flawed evidence led to 'mission creep'", *The Guardian*, 16/05/2000, http://www.guardian.co.uk/Archive/Article/0,4273,4018568,00.html.
Maslow, Abraham 1966: "The Psychology of Science: A Reconnaissance", Harper, New York.
Mearshimer, John 1990: "Back to the Future: Instability in Europe after the Cold War", *International Affairs* 15:1 (summer), pp. 5-56.
Meyer, Christoph O. 2006: "The quest for a European strategic culture: changing norms on security and defence in the European Union", St. Martin's Press, London and New York.
Miskimmon, Alister 2004: „Continuity in the Face of Upheaval – British strategic culture and the impact of the Blair government", *European Security* 13:3 (special issue), pp. 273 – 299.
Moravcsik, Andrew 1997: „Taking Preferences Seriously. A Liberal Theory of International Politics", *International Organization* 51:4 (autumn), pp. 513 – 553.
Müller, Harald 1994: "Internationale Beziehungen als kommunikatives Handeln", *Zeitschrift für Internationale Beziehungen* 1:1 (June), pp. 15 – 44.
Munro, Sir Alan 1996: "An Arabian Affair", Brasseys, London.
Murray, Williamson/Scales, Robert 2003: "The War in Iraq", Harvard University Press, Cambridge MA.
NATO 2003a: "Regional Headquarters Allied Forces Southern Europe Fact Sheet Operation Sharp Guard", 18/08/03, www.afsouth.nato.int/operations/SharpGuard/SharpGuardFactSheet.htm.
NATO 2003b: "Regional Headquarters Allied Forces Southern Europe Fact Sheet Operation

Deny Flight", 18/07/03
www.afsouth.nato.int/operations/denyflight/DenyFlightFactSheet.htm,
Noelle-Neumann, Elisabeth/Köcher, Renate (ed.) 1993: „Allensbacher Jahrbuch der Demoskopie", 1988 – 1992", Verlag für Demoskopie, Allensbach
Noelle-Neumann, Elisabeth/Köcher, Renate (ed.) 1997: „Allensbacher Jahrbuch der Demoskopie", 1993 – 1997", Verlag für Demoskopie, Allensbach
Paul, James/Spirit, Martin 2002: "Riots, Rebellions, Gun Boats and Peacekeepers", 2002, http://www.britains-smallwars.com/RRGP/EastTimor.html
Pflüger, Friedbert 1994: "Deutschland driftet. Die konservative Revolution entdeckt ihre Kinder", ECON Verlag, Düsseldorf
Presse- und Informationsamt der Bundesregierung 2006: „Verteidigungshaushalt steigt um 150 millionen", Press release, 23/06/06, http://www.bundesregierung.de/nn_22852/Content/DE/Artikel/2006/06/2006-06-23-verteidigungshaushalt-steigt-um-150-millionen.html.
Reuter, Jens/Clewing, Conrad (ed.) 2000: "Der Kosovo Konflikt. Ursachen, Verlauf, Perspektiven", Wieser Verlag, Klagenfurt
Rynning, Sten 2003: „The European Union: Towards a Strategic Culture?" *Security Dialogue* 34: 4, pp. 479 - 496
Schmidt, Peter 2006: „Freiwillige vor!", *Internationale Politik* (November), pp. 68 - 77
Schneider, Peter 1999: "Eiserne Mienen", *Frankfurter Allgemeine Zeitung*, 23/04/99, p. 43
Smith, R. Jeffrey 1998: "Officials Seek Kosovo Intervention, British Draft of U.N. Resolution Urges 'All Necessary Measures'", *Washington Post*, 6 June 1998
Snyder, Jack 1977: "The Soviet Strategic Culture: Implications for Limited Nuclear Operations" (R2154-AF, Rand Corporation), Santa Monica
Sozialwissenschaftliches Institut der Bundeswehr 2006a: „Einstellungen der Bundesbürger zu zentralen sicherheits- und verteidigungspolitischen Fragen", www.sowi.bundeswehr.de
Sozialwissenschaftliches Institut der Bundeswehr 2006b: "Forschungsbericht 84", www.sowi.bundeswehr.de
Stockholm International Peace Research Institute 2007: "SIPRI Data on Military Expenditure", http://first.sipri.org/non_first/milex.php,
Stürmer, Michael 1992: „Die Grenzen der Macht. Begegnungen der Deutschen mit der Geschichte", Siedler Verlag, Munich
UK Ministry of Defence 2007: "UK Defence Statistics 2007", data available online at http://www.dasa.mod.uk/natstats/ukds/2007/c1/table108.html.
UN Department of Public Information 1996: "United Nations Protection Force", 09/1996, http://www.un.org/Depts/dpko/dpko/co_mission/unprof_b.htm
US Department of Defense Technical Information Center 1995: "Operation Joint Endeavour Fact Sheet", 11/12/95, http://www.dtic.mil/bosnia/fs/fs006b.html
van Orden, Geoffrey 1991: "The *Bundeswehr* in Transition", *Survival* 33:4 (July-August), pp. 352 – 370
Waltz, Kenneth 1979: "Theory of International Politics", McGraw-Hill, Reading (MA) – London
Waltz, Kenneth 1993: "The Emerging Structure of International Politics", *International Security* 18: 2, pp. 44-74
Weiland, Severin 2007: „Tornados in Startposition", *Spiegel Online*, 26/01/2007, http://www.spiegel.de/politik/deutschland/0,1518,462492,00.html
Wendt, Alexander 1992: „Anarchy is what States Make of it: The Social Construction of Power Politics", *International Organization* 46:2 (spring), pp. 391-425
Wentz, Larry 1997: "Lessons from Bosnia: The IFOR Experience", Department of Defense Command and Control Research Program, Washington D.C

Williams, Paul 2001 "Fighting for freetown: British military intervention in Sierra Leone", Contemporary Security Policy, 22:3, 140 – 168
Williams, Paul 2005: "British Foreign Policy under New Labour", Palgrave Macmillan, New York

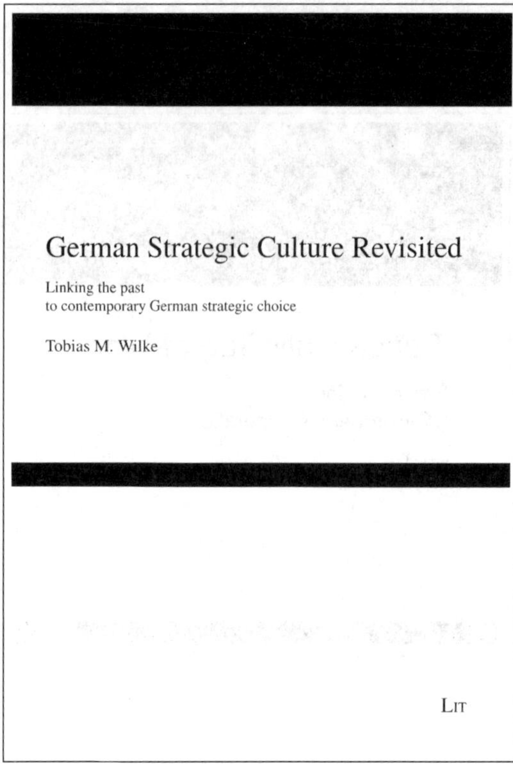
German Strategic Culture Revisited
Linking the past
to contemporary German strategic choice
Tobias M. Wilke
LIT

Philipp Meissner
The International Criminal Court Controversy
A scrutiny of the United States' major objections against the Rome Statute
The United States' opposition to the International Criminal Court (ICC) has developed into the epitome of fierce controversy concerning the international legal order in the 21st century. This volume represents an analysis of both the legal objections asserted by the involved U.S. administrations as well as a set of political motives the author considers likely to underlie their opposition. Fostering mutual understanding is the pre-condition for achieving an ease of tension in the future – which is in the very interest not only of the ICC and its States Parties, but also of the United States.
Bd. 33, 2005, 136 S., 19,90 €, br., ISBN 3-8258-8371-x

LIT Verlag Berlin – Hamburg – London – Münster – Wien – Zürich
Fresnostr. 2 48159 Münster
Tel.: 0251 / 620 32 22 – Fax: 0251 / 922 60 99
e-Mail: vertrieb@lit-verlag.de – http://www.lit-verlag.de

Caroline Fehl
Europäische Identitätsbildung in Abgrenzung von den USA?
Eine Untersuchung des deutschen und britischen Mediendiskurses über das transatlantische Verhältnis
Die Studie untersucht die These, dass in europäischen Medien eine europäische Identität in Abgrenzung von den USA konstruiert wird. Zur Messung dieser Abgrenzung gegenüber einer positiven Identifikation mit den USA sowie nationaler Unterschiede wird ein Forschungsdesign für eine quantitative Frameanalyse entwickelt, das auf Theorien kollektiver Identitätsbildung und konstruktivistischen Theorien der Internationalen Beziehungen aufbaut. In einer illustrativen Untersuchung wird das entwickelte Analyseraster auf die Berichterstattung ausgewählter britischer und deutscher Tageszeitungen angewandt.
Bd. 32, 2005, 128 S., 14,90 €, br., ISBN 3-8258-8136-9

Mareike Kleine
Die Reaktion der EU auf den 11. September
Zu Kooperation und Nicht-Kooperation in der inneren und äußeren Sicherheit
Die vorliegende Studie beschäftigt sich mit der Reaktion der Europäischen Union auf die Terroranschläge vom 11. September. Ausgangspunkt der Untersuchung ist folgendes empirische Puzzle: Warum kam es nach den Anschlägen zu einer erhöhten Kooperation der EU-Mitgliedstaaten im Bereich innere Sicherheit, während im Bereich der äußeren Sicherheit hingegen kaum Kooperation erfolgte und das, obwohl der 11. September als ein beide Dimensionen der Sicherheit betreffendes Phänomen begriffen wurde und sich die Staats- und Regierungschefs eine gleichmäßige Weiterentwicklung der entsprechenden Politiken auf europäischer Ebene zum Ziel setzten.
Bd. 31, 2004, 136 S., 19,90 €, br., ISBN 3-8258-8256-x

Joanna Lucia Bodenstein
Frankreichs Antwort auf das Ende des Ost-West-Konflikts
Die Reaktion des politischen Systems auf den Umbruch 1989
In Umbruchphasen der internationalen Beziehungen gewinnt die Sicherheitspolitik einen besonderen Stellenwert; sie beinhaltet Anforderungen und Gestaltungsspielräume zugleich. Der Fall der Berliner Mauer 1989 ist Symbol für das Ende des Ost-West-Konflikts und eine historische Zäsur, die Europas Sicherheitsarchitektur grundlegend veränderte. Diese Studie analysiert Frankreichs Handlungsspielraum nach dem Mauerfall zwischen Autonomieanspruch und zunehmender internationaler Interdependenz. Welche Politik verfolgte Frankreich gegenüber der deutschen Vereinigung, wie entwickelte sich Frankreichs internationaler Rang? Welche Antworten gab die französische Politik auf die neuen Fragen an die nationale Verteidigung und die Reform der Bündnisstrukturen? Wie reagierte Frankreich auf die gesamteuropäischen Herausforderungen, u. a. die EU-Osterweiterung?
Bd. 30, 2002, 344 S., 25,90 €, gb., ISBN 3-8258-5877-4

Michael J. Williams
On Mars and Venus
Strategic Culture as an Intervening Variable in US and European Foreign Policy
In 2003 the idea that Americans were from Mars and Europeans from Venus stirred up serious conversation about the nature of the transatlantic relationship on both sides of the Atlantic. While useful in prompting discussion, the introduction of pop-psychology terminology into IR lexicon was essentially divisive and not analytically helpful. Kagan relied on journalistic generalization, rather than tested academic methods to support his work. This study rectifies that deficiency, exploring the extent that Americans are from Mars and Europeans from Venus by deploying the analytical concept of strategic culture for an un-biased analysis of transatlantic drift.
Bd. 29, 2006, 112 S., 14,90 €, br., ISBN 3-8258-8134-2

Peter Barschdorff
Facilitating Transatlantic Cooperation after the Cold War
An Acquis Atlantique. Copublished with Palgrave, New York
Why are Europe and America still allied? After all, many observers predicted after the Cold War that NATO might collapse, trade disputes could escalate, and political relations would suffer in the absence of a common threat (like the one formerly posed by the former Soviet Union). Peter Barschdorff argues that an acquis atlantique is holding the two sides together. Common experiences, legal stock and understandings make decision-makers converge their views on controversial issues, such as peacemaking in the Balkans, NATO reform and trade of agricultural goods. The acquis might change over time. But as an analytic concept and as a driver of transatlantic politics it will remain an important constant.
Bd. 28, 2001, 256 S., 20,90 €, br., ISBN 3-8258-5434-5

LIT Verlag Berlin – Hamburg – London – Münster – Wien – Zürich
Fresnostr. 2 48159 Münster
Tel.: 0251/6203222 – Fax: 0251/9226099
e-Mail: vertrieb@lit-verlag.de – http://www.lit-verlag.de